Taking Care of Business

Taking Care

by DAVID VISCOTT, M.D.

# of Business

A Psychiatrist's Guide to Success

William Morrow and Company, Inc. New York

Library of Congress Cataloging in Publication Data

Viscott, David S., 1938–
   Taking care of business.

   1. Success in business. I. Title.
HF5386.V57   1985   650.1'3   85-4811
ISBN 0-688-04193-0

Printed in the United States of America

First Edition

1 2 3 4 5 6 7 8 9 10

BOOK DESIGN BY LINEY LI

For Bill Dockser

Acknowledgments ⸻

The author thanks Pat Golbitz for her editorial suggestions, Heidi Yorkshire, Maureen and Eric Lasher for their conceptual direction, and Liz Viscott especially for her editorial help and production assistance.

Contents _____

In the long run men hit only what they aim at.

—*Thoreau*

I. Introduction

You would be much more effective if you knew how to handle your business matters unemotionally. When your personal feelings interfere in business, they cause frustration, cloud your judgment, and lead to failure. You must keep your emotional distance to be successful. This book will teach you the psychology of winning in business.

No matter how humane your motives, you are in business because you want to profit from your efforts. In business, you work with other people not for friendship but because you want them to help you reach your goals.

If you are in business to achieve some kind of emotional gain, you will lose. If you make business people your audience, they can control you by withholding their applause.

Business behavior is measured rather than spontaneous. You pay for everything. Whenever you use a business situation to feel better about yourself, you give others an unfair advantage because in business, neediness makes you vulnerable. So, if you seek praise, people will praise you, not enough to satisfy you, just enough to keep you coming back for more. Emotions give your hand away.

You still must learn to walk the fine line between being friendly and being friends. Friends share the same vulnerability, while business associates do not. Business associates have their own interests at stake, not the other person's. Accepting this without taking it personally is the key to being effective.

Most of the people who are victimized in business set themselves up to be used. If you asked them, they'd be quick to point out how others were at fault, but what they'd really mean is that when they gave others an advantage, others took it.

Other people are not ruthless villains, they are simply in business to survive. If you expect others to look after your needs, you'll only be hurt and find sinister motives where none exist and confuse matters further. If you seek to blame or retaliate, you waste time and energy and reveal your weaknesses.

Succeeding in business should not be left to chance. This book will show you how to evaluate other people and will tell you what they really want. It will teach you powerful psychological techniques for dealing with difficult business situations, especially those where you are at a disadvantage. These techniques will help you maximize your strengths, lower your stress, see situations more clearly, and so act more efficiently.

This book will also help you understand how you get in your own way and what you can do about it. And it will show you how to make others feel they have won so that you can enjoy their cooperation and goodwill.

The choice is simple. You can learn to manage the business aspects of your life or you can leave success to others. You can pay outrageous prices for meaningless praise, or you can succeed on your own terms and be happy. You should have what you deserve and feel comfortable with it. This book presents a method for taking your plans and making them a reality so that you can achieve as much as possible and make your greatest contribution.

There's no point in having a dream if you don't have the techniques for making that dream come true.

II. Psychological Tactics

Chapter One _____

A PSYCHIATRIST'S TOOL KIT

_____

When I first began my psychiatric residency, I was surprised to discover that human behavior was not predictable and that there were no set rules for dealing with people or managing difficult interpersonal situations. Instead I learned a wide range of principles and techniques, some vague, some precise, but all easy to learn and apply. Sometimes the particular skill was an attitude, sometimes a direction. Understanding these skills and knowing when to use them can give you a significant advantage in business. For in business, like psychiatry, your effectiveness depends on limiting your emotional involvement. Most of these "psychological" skills depend on simple common sense and are already known to you. The chances are you have neglected to employ them because you didn't realize how important they were or because you doubted yourself. In fact, the most valuable skill you have is the ability to trust yourself and to follow your own common sense, because if you don't, none of these techniques counts for very much.

What follows here are essentials of a psychiatrist's techniques as they relate to business situations.

One afternoon at the start of my psychiatric training, after struggling with a difficult patient who twisted whatever I said and made unrealistic demands, I desperately blurted out to my supervisor, "What is a psychiatrist supposed to do?" My supervisor was a source of constant good cheer and support such as one meets only rarely in life. I admired him greatly and believed that he could figure out anything. I wanted to be like him. When I discovered that he brought Swiss cheese sandwiches for lunch every day, I brought Swiss cheese sandwiches for lunch every day, too. I was ready for his answer.

"A psychiatrist's goal is to understand," he replied.

"But what if you don't understand?" I protested.

"Ask questions until you do."

"It's that simple?"

"Let your natural curiosity guide you."

This was the best advice I ever got.

In order to achieve this understanding, a psychiatrist must clear his mind of personal concerns and become a dispassionate observer. It's not easy to get your ego out of the way in business, but it's just as essential as it is in psychiatry.

The most important rule is, Don't become emotional. You'll lose your capacity to deal effectively. Even if your job is at stake, or what the other person says about you is false, don't react emotionally, just be the observer. Ask questions that will identify points of common agreement and define conflicts. Ask others to explain their point of view. By allowing the other person to say what he or she really feels and thinks, you appear reasonable and strong, and become an ally.

Don't let yourself be injured by negative comments. Unless the words are "You're fired" or "No deal," assume that a solution can still be reached. Don't take anything personally. Your feelings don't matter in business. If you make them matter, then you will pay for it.

Your job is to observe with distance and then, once you know what is best for you, to act dispassionately.

You take distance to be able to deal effectively. When you take distance, your feelings aren't permitted to influence your decisions and you focus on seeing the situation clearly. If you don't have distance, your feelings determine what you perceive. Taking distance begins with accepting your feelings and personal problems as part of the way you are without making excuses or apologies for them. If you can do this, you are free to listen to other people without superimposing your problems on theirs. When you deny that you have problems or expect business to compensate you for the disappointments in your personal life, you are especially prone to lose your way. Understanding this and putting it into practice will do more to make you successful in your business relationships than almost anything else.

To do this, let the truth guide you. It is your most powerful weapon. Courage comes from the truth, from realizing the necessity of some particular action. Your objective should be to understand the truth of your and others' position. If you don't understand something, assume it hasn't been properly explained. Try to discover what is missing from the explanation.

Pursuing the truth gives you direction, shapes your method, and reveals the correct answers. As you search, be sure not to blame others. You'll only meet resistance. Instead, invite the other person to join you. Should others resist, it will be apparent. Gather your facts and note any discrepancies. Ask the other person to help make sense of them. Lead from curiosity, not from suspicion. Be open about your ignorance in order to get the most assistance.

Being yourself is always the best policy. Your feelings give you the best clues, and trusting yourself provides the best motivation. The sharpest trader, and the toughest negotiator, trust their feelings and are ready to admit they don't want to deal if the situation no longer seems in their best interests. In all their decisions the truth is their guide.

It should be yours.

When someone asks your opinion, simply reveal your thinking. Don't try to sell your version of the truth. Just relate it naturally. Don't allow your comments to be a put-down. You'll only cause hurt. The other person will only become closed, your opinion will be lost in the confusion and it won't be appreciated.

If you have to lie about what you believe, your opinion doesn't matter. Your opinion is valued most when it is direct. Still, there's no point telling the truth if all you'll gain from it is to offend others. Keep your goals clearly in mind.

If you know the other person is afraid of losing face, don't confront that person with his or her inadequacy. Use your knowledge to avoid causing injury carelessly. Let your goals dictate how much you disclose.

State only the information that is necessary to support your position. Don't try to demonstrate how brilliant or how worthy you are, or how wrong someone else is.

An honest opinion stands alone. It doesn't need you to do anything for it except to state it. It is where you hedge on being as honest as you can that others will question. Your doubting and qualifying point the way to your weakness.

If someone asks you your opinion of another person, try to get the question defined as narrowly as possible. What exactly does he want to know? Is he fishing for information? How will he use it? Don't be afraid to ask what he is concerned about. Be helpful, but don't needlessly provide ammunition to a conflict that is none of your business. Speak in as generous terms toward others as you can.

A good rule to remember is that you get treated the way you treat others.

Speak plainly. Say what you mean, just as you think it. Don't try to impress anyone. Be direct. Don't worry about who likes or doesn't like what you have to say. Whatever your contribution, speaking plainly is the best way to make it.

Don't agree with someone else's opinion just because you're

afraid to give your own. It's not safe to agree insincerely. You might be asked to defend your statement, especially if the original idea is a trial balloon.

Avoid jargon. If you can't explain yourself in simple terms, you don't understand what you're talking about. It's true that in some technological settings people are expected to use the vocabulary of the trade; however, the brightest and the best people in any profession speak simply enough that lay people can understand.

Get others to speak plainly by asking them what they really mean. You will always sound wise, and as they condense their thoughts they will teach you all they know.

Being open is not an excuse for being tacky, cheap, or cruel.

Express your idea as it forms in your mind, without editing. Don't try to make your comments perfect. Just be spontaneous.

Don't be afraid to say "I want" and "I need." Such comments are hard to ignore and have a striking impact.

Being open makes other people feel comfortable in your presence because it indicates you feel safe.

It's more appropriate to be closed while you survey the opposition and seek your strongest position.

Be closed in the face of hostility, when the other person is probing your vulnerability and looking for ways to take advantage of you.

Be closed when you feel frightened by a situation you don't understand, when you think you are being taken advantage of.

Don't leap into a strange situation. Running headlong into the battle may stun and amaze others, but more often it works against you. The times for acting boldly aren't that frequent.

It's wise to be closed when information is scanty. Just keep in mind that the people who are most likely to fail never seem to have enough information. Their problem is that they are too closed and postpone even necessary risks. When you act closed out of habit, it robs you of flexibility and spontaneity, and leaves you less able to protect yourself. Being closed works best for the moment, while you wait for your path to clear, but not as a long-range strategy.

Be closed with criticism, open with praise.

Be closed with anger, open with warmth.

Be closed with envy, open with admiration.

Be closed with resentment, open with forgiveness.

If you want to be open all the time and never hold anything back, you won't do as well. That's the way the world is. So be flexible, understand that your actions must be planned and use being closed to plan, not to avoid.

Admitting what you don't know can be a highly successful approach to unfamiliar business situations. It can lead to unexpected solutions.

A woman who had broad experience in publishing sought to expand one of her properties into an animation project. She had no illusions of herself as another Walt Disney, but felt that her concept and character had great potential. Rather than put the project in the hands of an agent, she decided to go into business for herself. She made appointments with the best animation houses in Hollywood and headed west. At each meeting she openly revealed that she knew little about the business, but thought she had a good idea. In one interview she was told that they did not take outside properties. At another she was coldly undermined.

Finally, at one company she was referred to an old-timer who had much experience, but little power. He spent hours with the publisher, telling her which ideas worked and which did not, where money was wasted, what the critical pitfalls were in dealing with animators and distributors, and how he would do it if he were starting a company from scratch.

The publisher met several other people who were also helpful. In each case, her openness about her ignorance created an openness in others. She asked questions about everything she didn't understand and gradually began to assemble the elements of her own animation house and went into business. Within one year she produced an animated Christmas special for television and won an Emmy.

Admitting your ignorance will get you further than almost any other tactic. Admitting what you don't know immediately puts those you're dealing with at ease. Finally, since your motivation is high and your interest keen, you'll be a good student and make the other person feel like an effective teacher. People can't resist that.

Flying blind, faking, is the opposite of admitting your ignorance. It sometimes works brilliantly. You can go to the podium, pick up the baton, and give a decisive downbeat. If you can carry off the proper attitude, the orchestra might follow. But what a game of chance! It's important to avoid being seduced into believing that if you act the right way you can get away with anything, that there is little in this world that requires special skill, or that no one really knows anything.

You can temporarily impersonate almost anyone in a position of control. If you convince others that you know what you're doing and seem to believe in yourself, you might even get away with It.

If you must fly blind, here are some guidelines for faking,

Ask for others' opinions, but don't give your own. Just say, "It's not quite right."

Always point out that you are still looking for the best direction.

Pose disarming questions like "How do you know that is true?"

State truisms vigorously: "I think we can do better, don't you?"

Get other people to express their self-doubts by asking "What if your calculations are wrong?"

Make few decisions. You can avoid being confronted by never making decisions.

There are times when you don't have all the vital information and must fly blind. This is what separates good leaders from ineffectual ones. You can distinguish yourself by making a decision when others are afraid to.

The effectiveness of successful business people depends just as much on others' belief in them as on their qualifications. Keeping this belief alive is what you must do to succeed and is especially crucial when you are flying blind. But remember, people who fly blind crash suddenly. Don't abuse the tactic.

Even if you must sometimes fly blind to provide the image of leadership under fire, your ultimate success in business depends on trusting your judgment and following your instincts.

People who trust their judgment succeed.

People who don't, do not.

If you want to lead, to create forward momentum and influence others, you must project a belief in yourself.

Herb, a brilliant businessman, came out of "retirement" at forty at the pleading of his brothers to take over one of the companies they had acquired in a complicated merger. The company he chose to run was poorly managed and was deeply in debt. It was purchased mainly for its tax benefits. The brothers were dismayed. They had hoped Herb would run the parent company, not the failing weaker sister. "Why this one?" they asked.

"Because I know absolutely nothing about the product or its manufacture," he replied. "It's a challenge. Besides, I can't lose. If I make a profit, we'll sell the company. If I lose money, there'll be more tax advantages. I think it's a perfect opportunity for me."

The brothers shook their heads and wondered whether they should have left him to his surf casting on Cape Cod.

On Herb's first day he toured the plant. Looking at long rows of complicated gray machines that filled a cavernous room, he asked incredulously, "We only make one product?"

"Yes," said the plant manager, a little disturbed at his new employer's ignorance.

"What does this machine do?"

"It rolls wire, a thousand feet per minute."

"It's huge. Why is it so large? It must cost a fortune to ship."

The plant manager shrugged.

Herb called a conference of his sales, marketing, and research people. It was his first meeting with any of them.

"Who's our competition?" he asked.

"There are five companies making similar products."

"Is there that large a market for this machine?"

"Why yes, and it's growing."

"What percent of the market do we have?"

"Twelve."

"How competitive are we?"

"We have a good product and our price is about the same."

"How many feet per minute does the competition's product roll?"

"They all range from a thousand to twelve hundred."

"And?"

"But, we're a better machine. . . ."

Herb waved for the others to be silent and went into deep thought. After a moment he turned to the head of research. "I want you to design a machine that will roll twenty-five hundred feet per minute, that weighs fifty percent less, is thirty to forty percent cheaper to purchase and easier to maintain.

"I want a complete cost analysis. Let's take a look at new ways of helping the customer finance purchases." He turned to his head of marketing. "I want an ad campaign planned around this new machine. We are going to create a product that everyone wants."

"But this is unheard-of."

"Exactly! If we had a product that was this good, cheaper, and easier to run, we'd capture the entire market. Why go for a product that's marginally better or a little cheaper? That's too hard to sell. But a product that is three hundred percent more efficient; that's an advantage that justifies getting rid of an older machine. I want the first plans on my desk in three weeks. I want to be retooling in three months and to be in the market-place in six."

"It can't be done," the chief engineer complained. "You don't understand the complexity of the problem."

"Of course I don't. That's what you are being paid for. I just know what is needed to save this company and your jobs."

In eighteen months the company had captured fifty percent of the market and enjoyed the brightest profit picture of any of the companies in the conglomerate, and to this day Herb doesn't understand the first thing about how his machines work.

In the final analysis, simple truths determine a business's success or failure. Figure out what's wrong. Don't look to blame. It gets in the way of clear thinking. Make a plan to set it right. Delegate the details. Trust your judgment and keep everyone on course. Real successes follow this plan.

You also need to avoid being manipulated. You can only be manipulated if you're needy. Most people need some form of love, power, or praise. Know what you need and you will be aware when people offer it to you. Then you won't be blinded by your need rushing to the surface and propelling you like a fish rising to the bait. You'll be able to stop and ask yourself:

Why is this person offering this?

How did this person know I needed this?

What does he or she hope to gain in return?

Do I really need this?

While these questions may seem to be born in the mind of a suspicious cynic who denies the goodwill of his fellow man, they are intended to give you an understanding of the manipulations that are designed to evade your knowing. People manipulate others by offering to fulfill their secret needs. The less aware a person is, the easier that person is to manipulate. The best way to avoid manipulation is to know your shortcomings and to take responsibility for them. Flattery is often the beginning of a manipulation, an attempt to get something by influence that may not be deserved, and so you tolerate flattery to the extent of your own insecurity. People who have real self-worth are bored by flattery and see it as a warning sign, alerting them to the time when the flatterer will approach and press for a favor. Be clear about this also: The flatterer who never approaches for a favor is seeking influence and power by association and is already using you.

People keep flatterers around to provide an environment that gives them a false sense of importance. This is all fleeting stuff with no lasting gain. When you permit flattery into your life, you only reveal your insecurity and sacrifice your integrity.

It's also important to know when to leave. Here are some guidelines:

Walk away when you realize you don't belong.

Walk away when the other person refuses to hear you.

Walk away when you are being provoked into a fight.

Walk away when the other person is out of control.

Walk away when you are being lied to.

Walk away as soon as it makes no sense to be there.

If you don't walk away when you know you should, you undermine your credibility and the strength of your will as well as your right to protect yourself. Don't walk away just to avoid painful situations, but walk away from those that are pointless, futile, draining, and unproductive. Once you have decided that walking away is in your best interest, do it and don't feel badly about it.

The key to interpersonal effectiveness in business is your integrity and willingness to trust your judgment. Nothing succeeds like confidence and nothing will give you more confidence than knowing the truth.

Trying to prove a point for ego's sake, putting others down, or being dishonest will always work against you. Being fair, giving your best, and caring about others is always the right tactic.

Chapter Two _____

YOUR
PERSONAL PROFILE

_____

Analyzing Your Strengths and Weaknesses

No one succeeds in business without understanding his or her strong and weak points. This knowledge is more important than any single skill or training. When people consider an experience valuable they really mean that it has provided knowledge that empowered them to take responsibility for themselves.

The following questions are designed to help you see yourself more clearly. Answer them truthfully, and simply, without altering your responses to fit what you think they should be. Your answers should reflect the way you really are. There will be a summary question after each section. Be sure to write it down so that you can analyze your profile later.

You don't need to record your other responses, just take time to answer them to yourself.

YOUR BEST JUDGMENTS—SUCCESSES

Consider all your successes.
What do they have in common?

What role did you play in each?

Were you a leader or a follower? Did you have close supervision or were you left on your own?

Were you functioning in a creative or a managerial capacity?

Did you work in a group or by yourself?

Did you do best in a particular location, in certain companies, businesses, careers? Why?

Were you on a rigid or free schedule?

What is the ingredient without which you wouldn't have succeeded?

What do your best judgments depend upon?

What attitude succeeds for you?

Looking back on these successes, why do you win when you win? Write down your response.

YOUR WORST JUDGMENTS—FAILURES

Consider all of your failures. Don't omit circumstances where others were to blame or the situation was out of control. If you were in business with a loser, it was your losing decision that put you there. If you lost because you didn't have enough information or the marketplace changed, it was your bad judgment not to ask or to be inflexible. It's always your responsibility to learn from your experiences.

You need to have as truthful a picture of your weaknesses as possible. After all, if you don't understand why you have lost in the past, you are most likely to lose in the same way again. Accepting your weaknesses is the beginning of real strength.

Do you see any losing pattern to your failures?

What were the most critical misjudgments that you made?

Did you misjudge people? Trends? To what extent did fear get in the way of your understanding? Were you overly optimistic because you were afraid to face the facts? Were you overly pessimistic because you were afraid of taking a risk and wished to justify your inaction? Are you still that way?

When you misjudge, what gets in the way of your thinking clearly?

What warning signs did you ignore?

When are you most likely to get into trouble?

Summarizing all of this, why do you lose when you lose? Write down this answer.

YOUR MAXIMUM VULNERABILITY

Let's try to discover your weakest point. Understanding and accepting your vulnerability is important, because it focuses your attention on the point where you are most likely to get into difficulty. You are most vulnerable when you do not know or accept this weakness.

When are you most likely to act in ways that aren't in your best interests?

How do people flatter you?

When do you waiver from what you know is right? When are you frightened, closed, defensive?

When are you most likely to lose sight of your goals? Where is your present business operation most likely to break down?

What personal failing gets in your way?

In summary, what is your Achilles' heel? Write down your answer.

SKILLS YOU NEED

If you could have any additional skill, what would it be? This could be another language, computer literacy, managerial skills, psychological awareness, anything you feel you need that would enhance your success.

> **What difference do you think having that skill would make in your work and in your life?**
>
> **How difficult would it be to acquire?**
>
> **What is standing in the way of your attaining it?**
>
> **How important is it to your success?**

Put down the skill and indicate why you'd like to attain it.

YOUR STRENGTH

> **When are you your best and most secure?**
>
> **Why do people look up to you?**
>
> **What personal quality do you value most in yourself?**
>
> **Put down what you believe to be your greatest strength.**

Look at your responses in the five categories just presented. Do they accurately reflect you? What kind of person is this? Would you want this person as your employer, employee, or co-worker? Is this person successful, happy? In what way does this person need to grow? How comfortable would you feel betting your life on this person? You do, you know.

Now let's look at the answers some highly successful people gave to these same questions. These people are powerful and respected. Many are famous. They are all high achievers and, all together, they control assets running into the tens of billions of dollars. With few exceptions they are multimillionaires. Examining their unedited replies will help you understand success. Comparing your responses to theirs will give you special insight.

The first case is a study in balancing belief in onself with the potential for self-deception.

WBD creates real estate investment opportunities by publicly raising money, obtaining federal loans, and then building and managing properties. He has built over ten billion dollars' worth of properties in the past ten years. A devoted family man, who at the time of the interview was awaiting delivery of his lifelong dream, a seventy-five-foot sailboat.

Why do you win? "Prudent optimism."

Why do you lose? "Believing my own bullshit."

Achilles' heel. "Dealing at too great a distance from people involved in my properties."

Desired skills. "Contemporary computer technology. Also, I wish I were more interested in people as people. It's hard to do in volume."

Strengths. "Judgment, trusting my experience. The ability to tell what information is responsible."

This man takes complete responsibility for his own judgments. His responses were instantaneous and his focused energy was obvious as he closed the interview saying, "I've got to go now. Go make a dollar." "Prudent optimism" describes exactly his business attitude. He believes in his inevitable success, and stays keenly aware of his capacity for self-deception. His perception of his vulnerability is wonderfully clear. Managing hundreds of people scattered widely around the world, he needs to be able to discriminate between what is real and what he wishes to believe. His desire for better computer skills and for more of an interest in people are again a reflection of his wish to have greater understanding for evaluating information.

* * *

This next case reveals a tug-of-war between intuition and overreaction.

MW is the president and chief executive officer of a major corporation that does over $800 million a year in sales and is enjoying dynamic growth under his leadership. An excellent decision maker, administrator, and planner, he is also a top negotiator who loves the game of business. A family man, pillar of the community.

Why do you win? "Intuition and experience."

Why do you lose? "Bad information. I trusted the wrong people."

Achilles' heel. "Overreaction."

Desired skills. "Greater ability to motivate people."

Strengths. "Ability to deal with people."

This leader trusts his experience and judgment. Because he sometimes uses his powerful negotiating skills to manage people, others may be intimidated in presenting information to him. Then he is forced to use his intuition to fill the gaps in his knowledge. His reason given for losing, however, reflects a need to blame others rather than take full responsibility for evaluating his information. This explains his tendency to overreact when things go wrong. His directness in admitting his weakness keeps it from being fatal. Desiring more ability to deal with people reflects this awareness.

This money manager walks a narrow line between patience and impatience.

DLB manages over ten billion dollars in investments in several mutual funds that he founded. He created a new method of indexing investments. He is internationally respected as a theoretician and strategist, and also for his practical application of investment knowledge. He is divorced, and currently building a New Guinea hideaway.

Why do you win? "When I can carefully phrase a question so that I and everyone else can understand it and I can document evidence that points to a single answer so that I know that single answer is correct, then I know that the real answer lies elsewhere. This is the theory of rational expectations. Everyone acts in a single direction, thereby self-correcting the system so that what seems to be correct is not."

Why do you lose? "When I am impatient. Most things will be all right if you wait long enough. I lock in error by being impatient."

Achilles' heel. "Impatience. I enjoy dealing with the uncertainty of a challenging situation, which when solved I tend to move off too quickly."

Desired skills. "To extend myself to more people. I'm good in small groups, not in large groups."

Strengths. "Giving other people the confidence to do more than they ever thought they could."

This businessman is passionately concerned with the accuracy of his information and the factors that distort it. His responsibility is to know the truth and to understand why he believes it is true. He presents his impatience matter-of-factly as just another obstacle. He is grateful to have it pointed out when it interferes. He is equally impersonal when it comes to the shortcomings of others. If he can see distortions, he can deal with them. He is entirely nonjudgmental. He doesn't care what the truth is, he just wants to see it clearly and react to it dispassionately. His desire to communicate more broadly reflects his need to share his burden, even though he knows, and secretly takes pride in the fact, that he can't.

Here is an entrepreneur who is willing to trust his judgment and repair his misjudgments.

HC is the model of success. He is the chairman of the board of a conglomerate that controls seventy companies, including the one that manufactures the wire-rolling machine mentioned before. He runs several of the subsidiaries personally, but spends most of his time looking for new acquisitions and traveling for pleasure. A personable and likable family man who is restless and full of energy, he is willing to attach his interest to any problem, will solve it and move on.

Why do you win? "Because I put the round pegs in the round holes and get the right person for the right problem. I seek the best advice and get people to do their part."

Why do you lose? "I make mistakes about people. I judge too quickly. I sometimes overestimate a person's ability."

Achilles' heel. "I sometimes put the wrong person in charge. Then I have to wait and let it all go down before I step in and save it. The truth is, I take over companies full of losers. All I do is move them around. I give a guy on the assembly line a chance to be a manager if I like his ideas. Sometimes he'll rise to the challenge, pleased that someone finally believes in him. Sometimes not."

Desired skills. "I don't know how to answer that. I don't know if I want any other skills. You know, I couldn't get a job working for any of my own companies. I'm not qualified. They're all Ph.D's. Maybe more education, but that would probably screw up the operation. The truth is, everyone wonders why I have so much free time, but I'm hard-pressed to fill two hours a day with work. I suppose I could get a broom and clean up the office, but it doesn't make sense, so I'm always looking for new businesses."

Strengths. "I trust my judgment for making a deal. Tomorrow I'm driving to New Haven to meet with a man and I'll probably buy his company over lunch. People say, 'Why don't you bring your lawyer or your accountant with you?' What do I need them for? How can they decide for me? They'll put the fine points together later. They'd only get in my way."

This man's confidence and ability to act on what he believes is right are inspiring. He accepts total responsibility for his decisions. He is willing to be wrong. He takes risks boldly and encourages others to risk by giving them something worth taking a chance for. He loves making a success out of a hopeless cause. He sees business as people and has an uncanny instinct for getting the best out of those around him by believing in them. He makes clear decisions that are easy for others to understand. No one doubts his direction or his intent, even if they think his goal is impossible. He is willing to fail, to make a misjudgment, to admit it and come to his own rescue.

Here is someone who believes in what she is doing, but doesn't always believe in herself.

LT is an inventive publisher, a creative marketer, and a disarming negotiator. She is the one who, on her first attempt at running an animation studio, won an Emmy. She is known for her giving and supportive nature, people feel open with her, and everyone who meets her recognizes her as a special person. Divorced, she is an adoring mother, a loyal friend, a powerful ally.

Why do you win? "I develop an idea or product that I think is fabulous. Then, because I'm convinced it is terrific, I have no trouble getting other people to agree. I see this as a confirmation of myself."

Why do you lose? "When I am not thinking well. When I feel bad about myself. When I don't believe in myself."

Achilles' heel. "My insecurity about my own ideas. If I don't think big enough for them."

Desired skills. "Honing my perceptions of others."

Strengths. "Understanding others."

This woman deals with people from an unguarded position. She only works on projects she loves and so gives them her fullest attention. Her directness in analyzing business positions gives her power. She only wants to know what is in her path or see if there is a better direction. She never holds herself out as an authority or expert and allows everyone she deals with to feel as an equal in dealing with the problem. Her self-doubt propels her to seek out the viewpoints of others so that she can understand what they know. She is a supportive part of any project she believes in, even if she doesn't have financial participation. Her tactics expose her totally, but when they work she is protected by the truth and supported by everyone around her.

The following case illustrates how believing that you will find a solution gives you power.

MS is a partner in a highly successful executive search and management consulting firm. Starting as a housewife seeking financial shelter from a failing marriage, she applied for a clerical position requiring no skills, and prepared for the typing test the next day by taking out a book from the library and memorizing the printed keyboard. Noticing her awkwardness, the examiner asked if she had ever used a typewriter before. When she explained how she practiced on the printed keyboard, he hired her on the spot, exclaiming that if ever he saw a winner, it was she. He was right. In a few years she became her examiner's supervisor and left the company to form her own personnel organization where she gained respect for her practical understanding of the workings of organizations and the corporate mind and for acting on her intuition. She is divorced.

Why do you win? "Because I know how to go in the back door when the obvious solution doesn't work. I keep my goal in mind and convince others of my goal, and I let their obstacles to my goal be their problem."

Why do you lose? "When I don't believe in myself."

Achilles' heel. "Not believing in my position, not going forward with it."

Desired skills. "A better understanding of world economy."

Strengths. "Creative adaptability."

This woman offers another example of the importance of believing in oneself and of how fragile the balance can be between belief and doubt. She sees forward movement as her object and looks for outside directives when she feels uncertain. Her desire to understand world economy to help her make decisions is a reflection of this lingering self-doubt. She needs to remember that trusting her intuition and judgment are the strengths that got her where she is, while doubting paralyzes her.

Intuition is fleeting. This case reminds us that you have to play your hunches as they are or not at all.

HH is the founder and president of a rapidly growing suburban bank with a dozen local branches. Highly innovative and caring, he takes personal responsibility for most of his loans, conducting many preloan investigations himself. While he is a master at figuring out a profit-and-loss projection and establishing budgets, his greatest skill is in analyzing the character of the people with whom he does business. Trusting his judgment, he gives people opportunities that their balance sheets might not support. Other bankers study trends; he studies character. A loving husband, he is the father of seven children.

Why do you win? "Preparation and intuition. Experience in dealing with people."

Why do you lose? "When I second-guess myself and allow me to talk myself into different actions. When my first-blush reaction gets colored by second-party dialogue."

Achilles' heel. "Loyalty interferes with my judgment and causes a lack of objectivity."

Desired skills. "A real quality grasp of personnel, people, motivation."

Strengths. "Financial analysis."

Clarity and objectivity are this banker's tools, but compassion is his guide. In meeting him one is struck with the force of his interpersonal intuitiveness. That he considers his ability to read people his strength, and his inability to read them his weakness, explains his desire for a better grasp of human dynamics. One thing is clear: He recognizes that doubting intuition, the inner voice that brings immediate reaction, is hazardous. This banker is also able and willing to correct his intuitive misjudgments by using his power. While loyalty may be his Achilles' heel, he compensates for it by setting limits and acting forcefully when those limits are breached.

This is the profile of a top manager of people with great ability to recognize and respond to others' needs.

JT is a senior broadcasting executive who ran a national radio network and then, because he wanted more contact with people, relinquished the presidency to run his own station. A beloved employer, he gives the impression that he has time for every problem and wants to help, and is on your side. He is happily married.

Why do you win? "Because I'm interested in people and their support. I've found that the way to the top is through the concerted effort of the people around you. These are the people who implement your plans."

Why do you lose? "For selfish reasons, when I forget about the goal and start looking at what other people will think of me. When I'm more concerned with what I look like than what I am."

Achilles' heel. "Ego. When it gets in the way of a disciplined decision, I'm vulnerable. Image. When I forget that I'm not trying to please everybody."

Desired skills. "To see any situation from someone else's viewpoint."

Strengths. "Personal relationships, motivation. Ability to see people's potential and to work on that as a support."

This man is an example of the ideal executive. He sees himself as part of a team and his role as helping others give their best. At his best, his energy is channeled into supporting others. At his worst, he tries to get others to support his ego. He is always mindful of this. While he is devoted to people and enjoys giving to others, he is willing to be unpopular, to be impersonal and hard in order to take necessary and often unpleasant steps. He sees the enemy as his ego and his goal to combat it by seeing the situation from others' point of view.

Here is a creative artist and businessman who has mastered the delicate balance of using intuition without becoming bogged down in feelings.

TW is the creator of one of America's favorite cartoon characters and is syndicated in over two hundred newspapers. He has expanded this original creation into a business that includes dozens of sublicenses that bring in over $400 million annually. He is also the creative director of a Fortune 500 company, for which three years ago he started a new division, creating characters and product lines that resulted in over $2 billion in new sales. He is widely respected as an artist and creative catalyst. His identity is becoming so closely linked to his hapless cartoon character that they are beginning to resemble each other.

Let's look at his two successes separately—first as an artist, then as a businessman.

Why do you win? "My identification with others. Communicating to them and touching them."

Why do you lose? "When I allow my own priorities to get ahead of him [the cartoon] and do something that is not in keeping with his personality. Or when I'm trying to use him as an outlet for my own personal expression. I misuse him when I put words in his mouth, when I do a cartoon that ninety percent of the people won't understand, and I think, 'Damn it. This one is for me.'"

Achilles' heel. "Overwork, pressures."

Desired skills. "Legal expertise so I wouldn't have to associate with attorneys."

Strengths. "Being able to deliver provocative sentiments in a nonthreatening way."

We see that becoming emotionally involved in art has the

same potential for damage as it does in business. And yet the object of the artist is not to be inhibited by the fear of losing control. To the extent that he is cautious, the artist is not free to create. Playing it safe always fails. If you wonder why artists often seem temperamental or unstable, walking this narrow line may help explain it.

Looking at TW from a business point of view:

Why do you win? "Being fortunate enough to see and make a logical equation, that satisfies an existent need. Being simple-minded enough not to be confused by details. Being ignorant enough of the facts of the things you can't do. Forever asking, 'Why not?' 'What if?'"

Why do you lose? "Whenever I carried logic beyond the market mentality, to an excessive place. Within the simplicity of the original logical premise also lies a danger of overgeneralization. In my biggest mistakes, all my logic was right, but I overgeneralized an assumption and carried it to an extreme."

Achilles' heel. "Professional ego."

Desired skills. "Wish I could type."

Strengths. "Creative analysis, working with creative people, validating them and yet, at the same time, being able to sit in on a board meeting and function in that arena as well. I'm good as a go-between for corporate management and the creative process."

This man sees a "logical equation that satisfies an existent business need" just as he sees a creative notion. The risk of carrying a business belief too far is like that of losing control of an artistic idea. Both ideas need to be tested against reality to stay relevant. There is a delicate balance between personal vision and the limitations of the marketplace. If you try to make a business situation or artistic effort fulfill personal needs, you lose perspective, for when you relinquish control of your personal feelings what seems right emotionally may have nothing to do with what can work for the general public.

* * *

Confidence and overconfidence preoccupy this real estate developer and entrepreneur.

ML is a deal maker whose strength is defining areas of mutual interest between parties and linking them together. He creates unusual solutions to problems by helping people focus on common goals, instead of on their limitations. In this way he gets people to risk beyond their customary limits. He is currently divorced.

Why do you win? "I win because my desire to win is so great that my concentration level to solve the problem is greater than anyone else's."

Why do you lose? "Carelessness. My concentration breaks because of overconfidence. I don't give enough attention to details, because of family or other emotional problems."

Achilles' heel. "Overconfidence."

Desired skills. "A better education in the fundamentals of economics and a better mathematics background. A Ph.d. in economics would do nicely."

Strengths. "My ability to analyze the circumstances of the people that I am involved with and the problem we are dealing with and the interaction of the two. And the ability to break down those elements into their finest points so that each party understands the problem, their relationship to it, and has no fear and so can deal with the problem clearly, openly, and honestly."

This man's confidence is his salesmanship. He projects his self-belief into his ideas. It would be difficult to argue against him. His belief in his ultimate success is so great that he permits nothing to dissuade him. His strength comes from staying detached and seeing the situation as a problem in need of solution. When people are strongly opposed to his position, he does not quarrel, but accepts their view as a legitimate reflection of their need and tries to find ways to meet it. When parties are far apart, he continues to believe that a common solution exits and that with patience he will uncover it. Controlling his

47

natural tendency to be competitive allows him to reveal the solution as a common choice rather than trying to sell it as his brilliant discovery.

Although his object is to help others see common ground, he is sometimes the only one with that clear vision. And so when others lose faith in the project, he's required to increase participation. This drains his time and energy and limits the number of projects he can work on.

Surveying these profiles reveals that no one particular strength is more important than any other in achieving success but being open about your weakness, whatever it is, will keep you from failing. Believing in yourself, working hard, giving your best, and being willing to take risks ensure success.

Successful people want to know the truth and are aware that deciphering others' distortions is just part of dealing with people.

All of these successes know that dealing with business problems is dealing with people. They have a genuine desire to understand others' point of view and to motivate them. No matter how well they do this, they continually seek to improve their psychological understanding.

Although these successful people believe in themselves, their belief is never total and never arrogant. It is always tempered by an open and ready access to their faults. Without exception each one of them immediately identified their Achilles' heel and their reasons for failing.

Only people who have the strength to accept responsibility for their failures have the courage to succeed.

These successful people define the problem clearly and allow it to motivate others.

They do not blame.

The most valuable lesson of this study of successful men and women has been to discover that every strength implies an equal and opposite weakness. The weakness reflects the special sensitivity of these people just as much as the strength does. In fact, no true strength appears unaccompanied by its negative counterpart. The weakness and strength appear as part of the same trait.

Accepting your weakness confers humanness and accessibility on you and promotes a spirit of cooperation in those around you. Others feel free to tell you what you may not know. They want to help you because they feel worthwhile and purposeful doing so. Admitting your weakness allows you to question whether what seems to be the truth may be a self-deception. This openness builds the confidence of success.

It is curious that these people would have succeeded with or without any of the additional skills they wished for. Real success depends on the belief that one deserves to succeed. The usefulness of all other skills depends on this attitude.

How did your profile compare to the profiles of these people? How honest were you about admitting your weaknesses? Do you use your strengths to their best advantage? What personal traits betray you? Do you take full responsibility for your performance? How can you be better? You don't have to be perfect to be successful, but you have to be aware to be effective.

Successful people know how to inspire others. They know how to make their point, to get to the bottom of a problem, present their view clearly and help people work together. These skills depend on caring for people, regarding their feelings and point of view as valid, taking them seriously, and treating them with dignity and fairness. Understanding people gives you real power, because it is only through understanding and meeting the needs of others that you build loyalty.

Chapter Three _____

UNDERSTANDING OTHER PEOPLE

_____

Learning How to Read People

Everyone has some natural ability to read others. The most accurate way to evaluate people is to observe what you perceive without making a judgment. Just look and listen without prejudice. Be willing to accept others as they are.

Reading people depends on getting your own emotions out of the way. Most of the mistakes you've made in judging others can be traced to some personal need that distorted your thinking. Perhaps you pushed good people away because you were frightened to compete with them or you became involved with losers because you felt superior by comparison. However, if it is undistorted, your initial response provides the most accurate information about others.

Pay close attention to any negative first impression when you meet another person. This impression is an immediate, uncensored input, occurring before you have been "educated" by the other person to see them as they want to appear.

A negative feeling always means that you should be on guard

because something is wrong. You need to discover where it comes from.

Always take time to frame a clear impression of your first response, even if it is only to remark to yourself, "This is a needy person" or "This person blames others." It's also useful to write it down. Keep your initial reaction in mind when you see the person again. Ask yourself if it still applies. Is there more evidence to support your hunch? Were you mistaken? Why? Being aware of how you distort and also how accurate your judgments are will give you confidence in evaluating others and your skill will grow.

Your comfort in dealing with another person initially is the key to how your relationship is going to progress. If you don't feel at ease in dealing with the person and this feeling doesn't change as time passes, it is unlikely that you are ever going to be able to get down to the business of working efficiently. Too much will remain unsolved. If you now have problems dealing with someone and you happened to have a tape recording of your first meeting and replayed it, you would discover several subtle clues that foretold all of your present difficulties. Your first meeting is that revealing, that crucial.

However, you should be willing to change your first opinion, for example, to ascribe the other's behavior to being in a strange meeting, but you must still be aware of any pattern that you see.

Keep in mind that in the first meeting, psychiatric or otherwise, people will reveal most of the concerns that have been on their mind for years, pressing for expression. Unfortunately, once expressed in this first meeting, they are often forgotten.

Sometimes you don't think as clearly in the presence of the other person, because the other person's defenses have an inhibitory capacity that blocks you from asking about what you need to know. Take some measure of this silent barrier. It is an extension of the other's inhibition and tells you how closed he or she is.

If you find it difficult to stay focused on what someone is telling you, that person may be using a boring drone to ward off close scrutiny.

If after a meeting you notice that you have a lot of unasked questions, write out the line of questioning you would have pursued if you hadn't felt inhibited. Try to understand where these questions lead. This may provide the clue you are looking for. The next time you meet with the person ask your questions directly. Become more familiar with the questions and feelings you tend to inhibit during meetings with others and you will gradually become aware of them at the time they occur and you will feel more comfortable bringing them up.

Keeping a record of your first impressions will help you increase the accuracy of your judgments. Know what gets in your way. Try to determine if there is a pattern to the way you misjudge. Do you rush? Are you swayed by flattery? Does a particular need lead you astray, such as the need for acceptance or praise? Be aware of your weakness. The person who can operate in your area of need can control you.

Remember, everyone is prejudiced. The successful person understands how. The wise person understands why.

The Three Personality Types

While it is true that almost all people will reveal themselves if you give them a chance, it is also true that people fall into three basic personality types: dependent, controlling, and competitive. Everyone shows some characteristics of each type at different times and it is rare to find a pure type, although a person is likely to stay predominantly the same type all his life. People tend to be most alike when they are open and loving; but under stress, defending against pain, coping with injury and adapting to change, people are likely to respond in their characteristic emotional style. It is at such times that a person most needs to be understood and managed properly, for while saying one thing to one type may be helpful, it may make matters worse for another.

What follows will help you determine whom you are dealing with, what prejudices they have, in which situations they are likely to do well, and in which they are most likely to get into trouble.

It will also be useful for you to determine your own emotional style and consider how it distorts your perceptions.

DEPENDENT PEOPLE

Dependent people dread being alone and so other people figure prominently in their well-being. They are happiest when they are pleasing another person. They feel most damaged when they are rejected, and so want to get as close as possible to others to prevent this from happening. Their greatest frustrations are caused by the obstacles that keep them from getting and staying close to others. And yet they are the ones most likely to create these very same obstacles. Why would people who want to be close create obstacles to closeness? To avoid the risk of being rejected.

This is the bind of dependent people. Their constant conflict is that they fear losing what they have as much as they enjoy possessing it. If you understand this, you have the key to making them happy.

Their proper goal is to grow up to become more self-sufficient so that they will be less likely to be damaged by the loss of another person or that person's approval.

The dependent position expresses itself as: a need for someone else in order to feel complete, a fear of abandonment, and a need for reassurance. Dependent people want instructions and need to be led. They need to know where to get help, but often are so afraid of being rejected for appearing stupid that they don't ask when they get into trouble. They tend to become helpless, let bad situations get worse, and need to be rescued.

Dependent people under the right circumstances are the most reliable and content members of any work force, the ones least likely to cause problems when their basic needs are met. They need constancy of support, to belong and be regarded as family, and above all to be loved.

Anything that supports these feelings enhances their well-being. This includes providing job security, retirement benefits, insurance protection, family health and educational support, frequent signs of emotional appreciation, and continued reassurance that they are doing a good job and won't be replaced or fired. Their loyalty, when they are well provided for, is unconditional.

Physical signs of belonging are also important to them: a parking space with their name on it, a specific work area they report to, a locker or cubby they can call "home." They need a base from which they can relate to the world around them. They need to be continually reassured that they play an important role in whatever system they work.

Dependent people seldom work alone. They need firmly set limits. Even though they may test them, they want to know the rules by which their behavior is measured. Even small changes in schedule make them anxious. They fear that they may find themselves in violation of some rule and risk disapproval. Rapid change tends to paralyze them and they can become obstructionistic. They are masters at this. Moving frightens them. The unknown terrifies them.

They require supervision, especially in difficult situations. No matter how well they do their job, being left alone makes them feel insecure. That is what their dependency is all about. Don't underestimate the power of this need. If they lose contact with their leaders at a time of personal crisis, even trusted personnel are capable of letting loyalty slide and following whoever seems to have the capacity to lead.

When dependent people feel you do not care, you have lost them.

Dependent people need as much preparation and explanation of any change as possible. They need information so badly that they will invent their own rumors and believe them if they don't have enough to go on. When they are afraid, they focus on their fear and little work gets done. So if a change is planned, issue a written statement and/or a timetable to provide structure and prevent distortion. Give calm reassurance and ample opportunity to ask questions.

Dependent people are especially sensitive to certain words and tend to hear them out of context. Examples of such highly charged words include: laid off, not needed, useless, uncertain, closing, moving, and leaving.

Words they find reassuring include: definite, certain, unquestionably, optimistic, positive, necessary, needed, growing, and permanent. Bear in mind that any expression of ambiguity, uncertainty, or potential loss creates anxiety because dependent people tend to remember only that you said a certain word, and fill in the details to match their worst fears.

CONTROLLING PEOPLE

Controlling people are difficult people to manage. They are not free and do not want you to be free. They want to control you, write the rules, define the terms, give the directions, illustrate the points, check the figures, find faults in the logic, show where you went wrong, and prove they were right.

It's no surprise that they find themselves fighting battles. They meet frustration everywhere they go.

They seek influence. They like having people indebted to them. They need to feel important. They want to be the key person. They want to create and control the bottlenecks of the world. Controlling people are calculating, not spontaneous, and are afraid to be open because they do not believe in their own

55

lovableness or real worth. They try to control other people's opinion of them because they are afraid that if others had their choice they would reject them. Down deep, they fear being abandoned just as dependent people do.

Controlling people often display a lawyer mentality. They bring up points for the sake of completeness, are rigid, ruled by precedent, and so are likely to be limited in their creativity.

Controlling people have excuses for everything. The fault is always outside themselves. They want others to think they are perfect, to make up for their self-doubt.

Controlling people are often ineffectual in leading others for they manage by intimidation and manipulation not by understanding. Because they do not trust their own worth, they also find it difficult to believe in others, and so they do not inspire. While their authoritarian style may achieve progress for a time, their tendency to use people inevitably comes back to haunt them. Since controlling people are loyal only to the things that give them power, others do not feel loyal to them.

Because their self-esteem is so fragile, controlling people tend to blame others for their problems rather than accept responsibility for themselves. As a result they learn their lessons with great difficulty, usually only after they have suffered defeat. Unfortunately, they often feel unappreciated and used at times like this and still decline to look within or grow. This is when controlling people get depressed or, in a last desperate effort to avoid responsibility, claim that the world is out to get them.

Controlling people always worry about losing control because they don't believe in their strength and doubt their ability to recover. Of course they would deny this. They frequently go to great lengths to prove an obscure point using excessive logic, tending to get lost in their reasoning. Their underlying message is almost always an attempt to compensate for their self-doubt. They want you to know that they are good, in charge, important, powerful, smart, and right!

It's important to be sympathetic when you correct their mistakes. Point out how difficult the problem was that got the best of them and offer to work with them. Arguing with them is a waste of time. They have an answer for everything and will only rationalize their actions and resist your reasoning. Avoid a power struggle by not blaming or accusing. Just state that there is a problem and that it occurred in their sphere of influence and you just want to help them fix it. Be gentle because this simple point will touch their self-doubt. Remember, controlling people secretly fear that their system is flawed.

On the positive side, controlling people have an excellent sense of industry. Let them revise the filing or mailing system, develop an office traffic plan, a seating arrangement, a schedule, a profit-and-loss statement, or a projection for implementing a new project.

They love to project into the future, because it is in planning for the future that they feel they have the most control. They love to anticipate disaster and prevent it. They are naturally concerned with what could happen. What if? is the question that rules their lives. In fact, it can run away with them. They tend to get so caught up in what could happen that they sometimes lose track of what is actually taking place. They often have difficulty in assigning priorities and may worry excessively about a problem that is unlikely to occur, merely because they feel powerful in addressing it; while they may ignore a severe conflict that already exists, because it makes them feel uncomfortable.

Because they are powerful persuaders, there is a danger of them diverting others away from more important issues and draining their energy. So controlling people need to be carefully managed, monitored, and reminded of their direction. Your object is to channel their energy and to put it to your use. Reassure them that your goal is correct. Do this firmly. Say you are not getting what you need from them and then tell them exactly what you want. Measure their work against your expectations, not by their system. They can always prove to themselves that their system is working even when it is your major obstruction. It's the nature of controlling people to create a system and to put themselves in charge. Once they do, expect to struggle to change it.

A tire company hired a man to run its warehouse. He spent hours alone, creating a complicated storage system that only he understood. Because the system seemed to work efficiently, no one bothered to find out how it worked. When the warehouseman went on vacation, the company discovered that it couldn't locate merchandise and had to shut down. Even so, the warehouseman's job was secure because he was the only one who knew how the system worked.

Controlling people need limits as much as they need to set limits because they get bogged down in details. Whenever something goes wrong, they increase controls and this makes matters worse.

When controlling people feel overwhelmed, they can suddenly let a difficult situation deteriorate. While their character may seem to change dramatically, you are merely seeing controlling people minus their controls. Remember, all these controls would not have been present if they were not so afraid of revealing this disorganized side.

When controlling people begin to slip, they often search desperately for something that will make everything better and prove them right. They refuse until the bitter end to think that their system may have been at fault. You must step in before this point, for alone they can cause great damage. Anticipate this pattern and cut your losses.

In desperate straits, we are all capable of such self-deceptions. We seek the Oracle, but hear in his utterances what we need to hear. We ascribe effectiveness to our method when the most it has going for it is that it is familiar. We insist that our plan will work when it is plain to everyone else that it has failed. We beg for a little more time. All we want is a break. We grasp at straws as our desperation makes us abandon our logic.

Controlling people do not make good leaders at the top corporate level; they do well leading small groups, where they get personal feedback that keeps them from becoming isolated. Because there is something ridiculous about being so rigid, other people continually test and tease controlling people and this can create an abrasive atmosphere. Still, they need supportive contact with others, for left to themselves, they will hide behind closed office doors and retreat.

While controlling people are more loyal to their own habits than to the company they work for, their thought processes can be a marvel of organization and thoroughness. They are the masters of the left brain. They number all the top accountants and attorneys. Although they like to think of themselves as creative, they are more calculating than intuitive, more intellectual than instinctive. When they are emotionally secure, they function like excellent mental instruments, providing their service with detachment and efficiency. When they are threatened, they use their intellect as a barrier, and their thinking becomes self-centered. At such times they give convoluted answers, overcomplete explanations, and advice bordering on the far-fetched. While they may follow the rules to the last detail, their judgment often lacks all common sense, and trying to prove how brilliantly they are, they only reveal their confusion and insecurity. They forget that how smart you are depends upon how free you are from need.

In dealing with the controlling superior, remember his or her tendency to use you coldly and to blame all failures on you. When he gets demanding, ask him if he thinks he is being unreasonable. Help him correct his thinking. Tell him that the pressure he's creating is making your job more difficult.

Be polite and matter-of-fact, but be direct. Don't challenge him. Whatever you do, don't take his controlling personally. See it as his limitation. Keep your distance. Remember, you're a stronger, more stable person than he is. Who but an isolated, lonely, and unfeeling person would ever treat people like he does?

So don't let him intimidate you. Interview him. Keep him explaining. He'll see you as open and cooperative if you don't contradict him.

Controlling superiors are easily humored, because they cannot imagine that others do not take them seriously. Unfortunately, humoring is sometimes the only way you can deal with them. If you must humor them, do it carefully. Agree with them, but be sincere about it. Remember, you are reassuring them, not lying. Tell them what they want to know even if it is silly. Don't laugh or even smile at them. It will just infuriate them and if they are in control, you may find yourself being assigned a lot of tedious busy work for punishment. That is their specialty.

If you cannot tolerate working under a controlling boss without being affected by him, leave. The boss won't change and you'll just wear yourself out. There's really little point in staying, unless you learn not to care.

COMPETITIVE PEOPLE

People mistakenly label themselves competitive when they really mean hard-driving, self-reliant, or determined. The hiker who lives through two weeks lost in the wilderness and thanks his competitive spirit is really talking about his survival instinct. Early man survived. Modern man, adapting his survival instinct to win over others, competes in business. Living off the desperate energy of the survival instinct is exciting and may result in material success, but it also exacts a heavy physical and emotional toll. Living a competitive life is stressful and feels like you are at war. The happiest people are not those who compete but those who continually challenge themselves to grow into their best selves. Their stress is low because they do not worry about being beaten. If they have a sense of failure, it is in realizing their limitations. Their victory is in surpassing themselves.

There are many degrees of competitiveness. And just as everyone has some dependent and controlling traits, everyone is also competitive. Schools foster competitiveness. The sports we play depend on it. The world is largely a competitive place, but living your life on the force of your competitive spirit is chancy. Remember, the competitive spirit channels the survival instinct to do its work. Time uses up life energy and so as competitive people grow older they burn out and dread being overtaken.

Competitive people make up the backbone of every sales force, sports team, and marketing division. They love the challenge of pitting themselves against others, testing themselves against the record, beating last year's figures, or topping the performance of the previous person who held their post.

Competitive people want to be better. This is both their strength and their weakness, for in trying to beat an unworthy opponent they may not set their sights high enough and may not achieve their full potential. When competing with someone far above their ability, they may become deeply discouraged and mistakenly draw the wrong conclusion about their true worth. They want to be winners all the time, but it's an unreasonable goal. In the competitive game, someone always has to lose.

Mature people learn that their proper aim is to be their best, to compete with themselves, to find a nurturing way of life; but competitive people get most fired up when besting an opponent. They like victory and can be so swayed by its thrill that they lose perspective and then often have difficulty finding meaning simply by being themselves. Beating an opponent suits them better because it focuses their attention outside themselves. They need to be winners in the eyes of others, because their opinion of themselves depends on what others think. It is this need for recognition that propels them forward. It is also what holds them back because they tend to tailor their behavior to win praise.

Deep down all competitive people are insecure and need external reassurance. They have little peace of mind, for as much as they desire to win, they worry about losing. They may appear to be good sports on the surface, but they are deeply hurt by a loss and, while they may use the pain of that loss to motivate themselves, they cannot rest until they win again.

It is this relentless outward drive that makes the competitive person so valuable in business. This is the person corporations screen for, the one who will take the job seriously, the self-starter who will pound the pavement and set the standard for the entire sales force, the one who will find a way to beat the competition.

Competitive people in business, especially those who work for someone else, risk not for personal goals, but for a symbolic reward: money or praise, even if they try to portray their employer's goals as their own. Their emotional security lies in the hands of others. They are obliged to please. If they get the applause they seek, they call it a good performance. Such competitiveness takes a costly emotional and physical toll. The goal of managing competitive people is to help them find a balance between continuing to achieve and learning to please themselves. Competitive people tend to suffer as they get older. They are most prone to heart attacks, high blood pressure, and strokes. The reason for coming to such an anxious end has to do with the nature of competitiveness. While they may seek to improve their playing skills, to become better salesmen or negotiators, they are mainly focused on winning in the moment. They do not set personal long-term goals. Their rewards are now.

If an organization wishes to capitalize on its competitive people, it should be prepared to manage their stress. The most effective way to manage their stress is to change their life-style, but this usually is impossible. There is also a risk that competitive people's production will fall without external incentives. So while quitting the rat race to run a small inn in Vermont is a widely held secret dream, the object of managing competitive types remains to help them align their personal goals with those of the company without manipulating them. These people need to be listened to, supported, and esteemed, especially when performance is off. Pressuring them into working hard to prove themselves, and win praise, doesn't work after a while. There is just so much energy to go around in a person's life.

By and large, it's easy to manage competitive people. Reward them generously in words and pay.

Competitive people want attention, need recognition, love applause, feel insecure, fear failure, dread being embarrassed, want to be better than the other person, and need a goal. They need praise and need to hear, "Well done."

Even though competitive people often work well on teams, they secretly want to be the most valuable player. While their competitiveness is their strong point, it is also the source of their greatest pain when they fail. Their natural tendency to overvalue being first makes them perceive being anything less as being worthless. They need continual reinforcement for doing their best and to be reminded of their value. Some never recover from the realization that they won't ever get to the top. Because they are driven only by the hope of victory and have little, if any, preparation for defeat, losing—and that may mean being second out of a field of a thousand—has the capacity for triggering deep feelings of worthlessness and even depression. Losing, like winning, is overvalued.

To manage competitive people in defeat, help them find some sense of personal worth. While putting pressure on competitive people at a time of failure sometimes works, it is taking advantage of their vulnerability. They may get up off the mat and fight for you, but they really need time to recover and learn to rely on themselves to feel good. Struggling to please others may work in the short term, but after a while the competitive person becomes a consumable. Be sympathetic and willing to hear their self-doubts without getting alarmed or blandly reassuring them. Insincere efforts will backfire. Helping them accept limitations and encouraging them to believe in themselves in spite of those limitations, promotes true self-assurance and fosters real loyalty. When competitive people feel they have worth to you only as a top performer, they soon lose their effectiveness as the stress of always having to be best takes its toll. Consistency and reliability need to be valued as much as being a hotshot. Competitive people cannot remain effective unless they develop this broader view of themselves. They need to see their value as extending beyond the accomplishment of a particular moment.

Underneath the competitive trait lies a need to be taken in and cared for. Form a personal relationship with competitive people and help them feel secure. Drawing on their insecurity to motivate them works but misses the point. Competitive people do best when they are encouraged to motivate themselves and they work hardest for someone who accepts them even when they aren't performing at their best.

In the long run, the most humane system encourages the best performance. Everyone needs to belong, to make a contribution and feel worthwhile, and to develop a sense of security that goes beyond the fluctuations of daily performance. More than anything else, people are searching for some meaning in their work and life.

Psychopaths—Con Men

Understanding psychopaths is important even if you may have very few contacts with them because each time you do, you risk being taken. If you don't recognize them in time, you will be seriously damaged.

The way to deal with psychopaths is to trust your suspicions! If you feel any doubt about what anyone is telling you, express it at once. Psychopaths will almost certainly have a ready explanation. It will sound prepared. It will be! If you pay attention to your feelings something will still not sound right to you. Just ignore their answer and their logic and say, "Something doesn't make sense here." Ask them to repeat. They will speak quickly, glossing over critical details. Take your time. Ask more questions. Listen to their answers from a distance, clinically. See if you can discern the motivation behind their words. At some point they may question how bright you are for not understanding them. This is an old ploy. Don't say, "Skip it," and allow them to continue. If you don't understand what they are saying, it probably doesn't make sense. You need to understand everything they tell you. For example, if you put money into a scheme you don't understand, the part you don't understand will be how you lose it.

Remember, you will always have some feeling of doubt in dealing with psychopathic people. Pay attention to your doubt. It may be your only warning. Ignore your doubt and these people will move in and talk you into believing their logic. Psychopaths are liars. They will tell one lie and when you question them they will back it up with another. They will do this with a straight face and thank you for asking the question. They have no moral compunction about this. In fact, they have no moral sense at all. They believe what is right is what is good for them. They lie constantly just to keep their world in order. They are the freeloaders of life.

They do not care one whit about you.

Expect them to be lying, you will seldom be wrong.

You sometimes have to discover psychopaths indirectly, by their wake, by the disturbances they leave behind. They are slippery and cover their tracks deviously. They set up others to take responsibility for their mistakes. They trick people into trusting them and keeping silent. If you look closely, you'll discover that they always seem to have some kind of controversy going on around them. The people working with them seem troubled. Others often feel restricted by some secret agreement they have been coerced into and are afraid of speaking freely, like the people who were afraid to say the emperor was naked. Wherever they work, people waste time having to verify information because they always start rumors. They always claim to have some inside information that gives them power. In fact, they often structure their rumors in order to give them this power. They undermine authority, destroy team morale, and create an attitude of suspicion and blame.

If you hire a psychopath, you are in trouble. If you discover a psychopath and do not fire him or her, you are a loser. Accept this: They are saboteurs. There is no curing them. They will never confess the truth. They will destroy goodwill. They will use you. They will never care. They will never help you. They flatter. They convince. They talk pretty. They act pretty. And yet they are often well liked by everyone because they prey on people's needs for attention and understanding. They sniff out a person's weak place and play to it. They befriend the lonely, the downtrodden, the insecure, and the desperate. They seek out those who want something for nothing, who want the bargain of the century, the greedy, the insincere, and those lacking in self-confidence.

Some good questions to ask suspected psychopaths are:

"Will you please repeat that?"

"Will you put that in writing?" They hate this, but when they consent, look for a highly manipulative document that is vague on the precise issue you wanted spelled out.

"Are you telling the truth?" Always good for shock value.

"Why are you offering this to me?"

"Who else did you show this to? What did they say? Can I have their telephone number?" If the contact is offered, make the call and see if the other person corroborates the information exactly. Remember, psychopaths set up everyone. Ask the contact how long they have known this person. Think about how they could have been set up.

Psychopaths love using pressure. When they do, stall. Say, "Let me think this over." Take your time. Ask your accountant. Tell them you want to talk to your lawyer. Watch their reaction. It will be very smooth, but you'll feel their discomfort. See if you can repeat their pitch convincingly to another person. If you can't, it means that the original presentation lacked something that their style conveyed.

That style is your enemy. It blinds you by dazzling you with praise and appreciation. Remember, psychopaths know what you need. They are the ones who will give you the most sensitive compliments. They will be the ones you will feel like befriending. You will feel that they are genuine. That they really do see you as you see yourself. Even when they are genuine they are studied. Their praise serves their purpose. You'd do best to thank them for their appreciation and let them go. Assume you owe them nothing. You don't owe them a thing.

Once you have found a psychopath, get rid of him.

Take time to absorb the material you have just read. It's a good idea to reread it in sections before and after you deal with a particular person. Since everyone possesses all three of the traits described above, it may not be possible to classify someone exactly. This material will still be useful in explaining dependent, controlling, or competitive behavior even if the person who is exhibiting it doesn't fall precisely into one distinct category. In general, dependent behavior will center around the issue of love, controlling behavior around power, and competitive behavior around self-esteem.

The main point about being an effective people-person is to care for other people, to understand them and help them fulfill their needs, not to use them or take unfair advantage of them.

These guidelines are intended to form a base for understanding how to deal with people in the special situations that will be discussed in the remainder of this book. Whether you are conducting a meeting, interviewing, or negotiating, understanding what is important to the other person and how it influences his or her behavior will make it possible for you to avoid unnecessary conflicts and will define areas of mutual agreement.

A COMPARISON OF THE THREE TYPES OF PEOPLE

	DEPENDENT TYPE	CONTROLLING TYPE	COMPETITIVE TYPE
First Impressions on Meeting Them			
Initially they seem to	Stress their worth and express their needs	Flex strengths, intellectual, and financial	Impress, brag or boast, display credits
And you feel	Nagged at, pulled, clung to	Unfree, rules and expectations abound	Like you are being sold something
They secretly feel	Incomplete by themselves	Flawed, out of control	Unsure of their worth
They want you to	Love them	Respect their power	Appreciate them
Driving Forces			
They need	To be loved	To be in control	To be best
Goals	To belong	To own	To win
Want from others	Loyalty	Obedience	Approval
They love	People	Power	Esteem
They envy	Adored people	Power	Fame
Possessive of	People	Controls	Limelight

	DEPENDENT TYPE	CONTROLLING TYPE	COMPETITIVE TYPE
Positive Features			
Strengths	Team player	Details	Self-starter
Work best when	Supervised	In charge	On top
Corrective goals	To be independent Needs to test self and grow	To be free Needs to let others be themselves	To love self as is To improve self
Support by	Reassurance	Respect	Applause
Desired praise	Good contribution.	Good control.	Well done.
Want to hear	You're lovable.	You're right.	You're the best.
Negative Features			
Weakness	Feels helpless	Feels powerless	Doubts worth
Potential problems	Avoids responsibility	Too rigid	Takes all the credit, big ego
Others respond by	Teasing	Defying	Putting them down
At worst when	Abandoned	Not taken seriously	Feeling limited
Correct advice	Decide for yourself.	Remember the goal.	Be your best.
Undermine by	Threatening to leave	Thwarting their system	Ignoring or denying their worth
Buzz words	You're unlovable.	I'm leaving you. You're out of control. You're wrong.	He's better than you. You're not so hot.

	DEPENDENT TYPE	CONTROLLING TYPE	COMPETITIVE TYPE
Defensive Positions			
Fears the loss of	Love	Power/control	Esteem
Dreads	Abandonment	Shame	Embarrassment
Main Defense	Denial	Excuses/ blaming	Pretending
Typical action	Clings sullenly	Withholds, explodes	Acts out impulsively
Manifestation of Stressful Feelings			
Anxiety (Threat of loss)	Panics, addiction, afraid to look	Becomes rigid	Pushes on till he/she burns out
Hurt (Sadness of injury)	Feels sorry for self	Self-righteous display of pain (guilt producing)	Resentful
Anger (Reaction to hurt)	Smolders	Seeks revenge, is unforgiving	Acts out dramatically
Guilt (Inward anger)	Physical symptoms, clinging	Silent remorse alternating with retaliatory wishes	Self-destructive behavior, often histrionic
Depression (Drained by guilt)	Overwhelmed	Overwork, bitter, stuck in rut	Dissipation of energy, no purpose
Life lesson	You are complete. Be independent.	You are responsible. Be free.	You are enough. Be yourself.

III. Communicating with Others

Chapter Four _____

FACE TO FACE

Getting Others to Say What They Mean

It is remarkable how much you can learn simply by asking obvious questions and inviting other people to tell you what they know. Be straightforward. Ask questions like "What's really going on here?" "Tell me what you think went wrong?" or "How did this happen?" Although some people will be guarded, most people are relieved by answering such direct questions.

To get honest feedback: welcome the truth, don't attack people for bearing bad news, praise frankness, and appreciate honesty, no matter how damaging it may be. Speak the truth without attaching blame or implying ridicule.

View the truth with the same detachment with which you would examine a navigational problem. You need to know your present direction and speed. Knowing all the reasons you are off course may or may not be as important right now. Some winds and currents cannot be anticipated, only compensated for. Your goal is to assess the facts and make the proper correction. Your faithfulness to the truth determines your success.

Continually monitor your results and evaluate the reliability of those you depend upon. Keep others focused on determining the accuracy of their facts.

People tell the truth to those who can handle it. People lie not merely to conceal their ignorance and errors, but also to avoid the reaction of someone who explodes, overreacts, or blames. The truth others tell you is the truth you can tolerate hearing. If you listen to the truth calmly, with understanding and curiosity, you will be told much more than a person who dreads terrible losses. If the attitude of those around you is "Who is going to tell him?" you have created the atmosphere for failure because you'll seldom learn about potential trouble in time to prevent it. People will make excuses why they didn't tell you. The real reason you didn't hear the truth is that you didn't create a climate for telling the truth.

CLUES THAT TELL YOU WHEN SOMEONE IS LYING

Your mere suspicion that someone is lying is evidence. Treat it as such. The more you feel you are being lied to, the greater the probability that it is true.

Ask yourself why you feel lied to. Listen to the answers that occur to you. Take them seriously. Share your concerns openly. Say, "This doesn't feel accurate," "What aren't you telling me?" or "This doesn't sound right." Watch the other person's response.

Being open with your natural responses is an excellent way to catch a liar.

How to Hold a Meaningful Discussion

MAKE AN AGENDA

If you expect to get something accomplished in a meeting, list your expectations and put them in order. That's your agenda.

An agenda doesn't have to be formal to be effective, but you need to have some plan in mind when you deal with others, to maximize your efficiency. If making an agenda sounds a bit contrived, remember that people who succeed make plans. You need to think of every discussion as a step toward your goal, so each step deserves careful planning. If the steps do not reflect the goal, they won't help you reach it.

PREPARING OTHERS

Give others time to prepare for a meeting. Tell them its purpose. This lowers their anxiety and increases their effectiveness. If you are unable to give people time to prepare, state your purpose at the beginning of the meeting and give them some idea of what you are expecting.

If you discover you are dealing with an anxious person, don't ignore it, be reassuring. Keep in mind the three main types of people and their particular concerns and address them specifically. You prepare best by making them feel safe. Only then can they concentrate on the problem.

There's no point in trying to talk if the other person is so afraid that he is not able to hear what you are saying. You always have to help other people to hear and see. You become easy to talk to by caring.

BEING DIRECT

Introductions should be brief.

Reassurances should be generous, appropriate, and effective.

Instructions should be clear.

Directness is a virtue. Whenever you can speak right to the point, do so. People always value someone who is direct. Skirting around an issue, either because you don't want to hurt someone else's feelings or are afraid of revealing something unfavorable about yourself, is always a waste of time.

Say what you want to say just as you want to say it.

Again, be brief.

Ask for the other person's opinion.

Correct any mistakes you make as soon as you make them.

If you have a new understanding, share it.

If you don't understand something, ask.

Do not be attached to any belief.

You are looking for the best answer, the solution that works. Everything else is unimportant. It doesn't matter that you are right, smart, vindicated, or others defeated. The only thing that matters is that you find a higher level of the truth and accept it.

WHEN OTHERS MONOPOLIZE THE CONVERSATION

When someone monopolizes a conversation, don't be hostile, be curious. Lead him to discuss his own shortcomings. Ask him difficult questions such as whether he could have done better, and why he failed. His own natural defensiveness will inhibit him. Eventually he will see that he is getting into trouble and will be grateful to be silent.

WHEN OTHERS ACT INAPPROPRIATELY

When someone acts emotionally in a business situation, he is acting inappropriately. Recognize the person's pain and allow him to express it, but do not permit yourself to be a target, allow your feelings to be hurt, or be trapped into fighting back. The other person's inappropriateness is no excuse for you to get out of control.

Responding emotionally in a business situation is always wrong and gives others an advantage. Resist angry provocation. When others reveal their anger, acknowledge it calmly. Focus on their grievance. Ask them how they feel damaged. This goes right to the heart of the anger and defuses it. Don't challenge any of their points. Don't be intimidated. Admit what responsibility you must, but do so in a businesslike manner. Don't defend yourself. Analyze the attack. Ask them why they are getting so emotional. Ask them what they want. Make it their problem. Rise above it. Do not react emotionally to an emotional outburst. Take control by assuming a positive resolution to the situation and by asking for constructive suggestions.

ENCOURAGING IDEAS

It's important to remember that even great ideas had problems at the beginning. It's easy to cut down any idea in the bud merely because it is new, hasn't been thought out, and has flaws. It is easy to be the critic, find fault, and kill initiative and invention, especially when you have power. Building an open atmosphere that inspires confidence and enthusiastic participation takes real skill and character. If you want other people to share their new ideas and be open, you must be generous and encouraging, not envious and greedy. Avoid discouraging people even when their idea is a dud. Praise them for their efforts and admire their searching, creative ways. The next time they may have the solution you've been seeking.

If you approach all new ideas as possibilities in need of further development, you have the right attitude. Become the champion for what works best. Recognizing and encouraging a good idea deserves just as much credit as the idea itself.

HELPING OTHERS FOCUS

Directing others is a knack. Although nothing helps others focus as much as being focused yourself, here are some questions to show the way. "What is the problem?" "How did you discover it?" "What does this all mean?" "Why are you telling me this?" "What do you think will happen next?" "Can you summarize this for me?" and "What is the next step?"

Your comments should always imply a forward direction, a profitable solution.

WHEN OTHERS REFUSE TO TALK

When you must have a "conversation" with a silent or sullen person, try to be prepared beforehand, and ask direct questions that clearly define what you are seeking and limit the painful interchange. Thank the person and be done.

When someone won't speak, don't make an issue of the silence. Accept it as the person's response. It means no. Indicate that you are treating it as such and give the person an opportunity to respond. Be silent for a while. Feel the space between you from a distance. Consider what it must be like to be the other at this moment. What would you want someone to do or say to you if your places were reversed? Restate your impression of the meeting and ask if that is the impression the person wanted to make.

Be pleasant. Do not respond to silence by being hurt or angry even though the silent treatment makes one uncomfortable.

There is no general way of getting people to respond when they don't want to. Silence is a defensive posture. Avoid trying to force people to talk; you risk behavior as manipulative as the silence that provoked it.

Try to set others at ease and speak to their unspoken fears, but if this doesn't work, being direct and limiting your exposure to their negativity is all that's needed.

MAKING SURE YOU UNDERSTAND WHAT OTHERS SAID

This is an excellent tactic, providing you do not use it excessively or to conceal yourself. Ask people to repeat anything you are uncertain about. Ask them to explain, to qualify, and to expand.

When people repeat, they almost always alter what they say. This can lead to fortuitous discoveries. So pay attention. Getting people to repeat is a good way to make a point without

angering the other party. Don't be afraid of asking others to repeat a point even if it is against you. Showing your willingness
to hear criticism enhances your stature. Thank the person for
his view. Show your appreciation for being corrected.

Getting others to repeat a point that is obviously false or
mistaken can be abused if you use it to ridicule others. Don't
gloat over others' errors. You don't need to be right at anyone's expense. Be grateful because they made a mistake you
don't have to repeat. Use the opportunity to clarify the problem, not to put them down.

CONCEDING YOU WERE WRONG

Conceding you were wrong shows your flexibility, openness, and
willingness to grow. It also empowers others by permitting them
to have a helpful impact on you. Allowing others to help you
creates a positive atmosphere. Accepting blame, admitting error, taking responsibility, all build goodwill and trust.

When you are wrong, admit it with the same detachment
with which you would admit being mistaken about the weather
and getting caught without an umbrella. No one will make fun
of you or add insult to injury. You're already soaking wet. But
if you blame the forecasters, or someone else for borrowing your
umbrella when it's clear you wouldn't have remembered to take
it, you'll become the butt of jokes and your being wet will only
spawn derision, not sympathy.

Conceding error is always a sign of strength.

Admit your mistakes as soon as you notice them. Accept
that you are not perfect. Realize that the attitude you show in
admitting your mistakes sets the example for others. Concede
when you have lost, by accepting the rightness of the new information. Be glad to be headed in the right direction again.

To win an argument without alienating others, realize that
the purpose of all discussions is to come to a higher understanding. If you insist on winning over others, you will lose.
Reaching new understanding is winning.

The way to win an argument is to avoid having to win the argument, but rather to see it as a continual redefining of goals and mutual interests. Don't insist on coming out on top. Focus on having your needs met and interests taken seriously and responded to.

Don't insist on answering every question or solving every problem. A cooperative start is also a victory. Some problems have to be endured. Some go away on their own. Knowing which battles to fight and which to avoid is more valuable than trying to win every point.

Sometimes you lose just by becoming involved in a fight. Some victories are empty. Sometimes you win best by helping the other person achieve victory. If you have to win by having someone else lose, your victory is diminished by the loss of stature you suffer in doing so.

Chapter Five

USING THE TELEPHONE EFFECTIVELY

The telephone can be your salvation or your undoing.

If you call with sensitivity and openness, the telephone is an effective investigative tool that measures the emotional atmosphere in distant places. It is a powerful communications device that can reassure a frightened associate, or give just the right input to close a deal. It extends you into the world, and multiplies your effectiveness.

Yet, if you call with fear and are closed, the telephone conveys your insecurity and undermines you. In a single call you can create a negative impression, undo years of goodwill, or break a friendship. It is both powerful and precarious. Because visual clues such as facial expression are missing while the potential for intimacy is increased, under stressful circumstances it's easy to misread others, project your own fears, and make mistakes. Misusing the telephone always makes matters worse.

The telephone is as sensitive and as subtle as you are. It magnifies your impact or it destroys your credibility. It accentuates your subtlety when you call at just the right moment with the right comment, but when you call at the wrong time, or are even a little pushy, it makes you out to be insensitive and crass, revealing your motives and magnifying your fears.

It's important not to get carried away with overanalyzing who should call and when. Too many businesspeople neglect to follow up because they don't want to lose leverage by seeming desperate. There is often considerable truth to this position. In the world of show business, there is a big difference between calling someone and someone calling you. The caller is seen as asking for something, empowering the receiver. Try to avoid getting caught up in such "rules." Let your instincts guide you. Too many opportunities are lost because a would-be caller has overanalyzed himself out of making contact.

It is important to develop a natural telephone style, one that is most like you, and permits you to be your best. Some people are inhibited on the telephone and have difficulty calling. Others who are insecure about their physical appearance or by the presence of others won't take no for an answer and can persuade on the phone well beyond their customary ability in person. They are braver at a distance.

When you hang up, the other person is left with the impact of your call. You have no more input, no more selling or persuading, no charming smile to carry on for you. The other person is alone with his or her thoughts and impressions, so it's important that your call works for you. You can increase your effectiveness on the phone and develop your telephone personality to serve you. You want to project strength. Know what setting makes you most comfortable to talk in. Be free of distractions. Concentrate. Don't read the mail or carry on another conversation in sign language. Take the time to be focused. Know what you want to say. Know when you want to hang up, before you call.

You need to assess the situation of the person you are calling as quickly as possible. Ask if this is a good time to call. Is there a better time? Be flexible, patient, and understanding. Remember, independent of anything you say or do, your call can be perceived differently, depending on the other person's situation. When someone has had a harassing day, your well-intentioned, but casual call might not be seen as welcome. The most important telephone skill is knowing when to talk or call back.

Evaluating Your Telephone Effectiveness

For the next week, including weekends, after each call, ask yourself the following questions. You don't need to write down your answers, but keeping a record of any kind will help.

Was the call necessary?

Why did you make or receive it?

Was the call too long?

How long did it take to get to the actual business of the call? Why?

How could you have made the call shorter?

Did you accomplish what you wanted? Why or why not?

How could you have made the call more effective?

If you could have hung up sooner, you were on too long.

If you hung up without making your point, you wasted your time.

How much time do you waste on the phone? Talking excessively in business is almost uniformly a bad trait. The more said in the least amount of time the better.

How many calls do you take a day? What time of day are you called most? Are you prepared to talk then or are you busy? Figure out when you receive the most calls and plan to be available then. Calling back is a waste of time and often you miss opportunities.

How much do you use the telephone as a leisure instrument during work hours? Everyone calls friends for a laugh and checks in on mother to see how she's doing. This is all fine providing you use the calls to feel good and keep them short. Calls to spouses or lovers fall into this leisure category, but such calls run the risk of adding stress if you discuss problems or fight.

Do you use the telephone to keep from working? Do you use the telephone as a safety valve, as a way of avoiding something? When are you most likely to call?

What impact do your calls have on those who receive them? Are they to be taken seriously or are they just recreation? If you routinely take unnecessary calls, you diminish yourself in the eyes of others.

I can claim a certain degree of expertise in reading people's emotions over the telephone from evaluating thousands of callers on my radio talk show. I'd like to pass along some of my secrets to you.

Listen carefully to what the other person says and to your reaction. Be calm. You'll have all the time you need if you don't rush.

Everything that happens on the telephone between you and the other person is important. Every emotional clue is significant.

A pause in the middle of a thought indicates hesitation. Follow the thought to conclusion in your own mind and you will have some idea of what the person was reluctant to express.

A cough indicates discomfort. It may be a fear of expressing disagreement or anger. Try to remember the subject that preceded it. The other person finds it threatening. Understand why.

A hand over the speaker muffling the sound is an attempt at censorship, revealing a fear of embarrassment.

A sigh indicates the perception of a loss. It may indicate a trivial dissappointment or reveal a deep hurt being concealed just below the surface. Or like a yawn, it may indicate boredom.

Any repetitive sound, such as "You know," suggests an automatic way of dealing with anxiety and may also indicate that a person is unwilling to be open.

Be aware of the context in which nervous laughter occurs.

Notice when others forget or lose their place. It often indicates that there is something they don't want to discuss.

Use all of these clues to shape your questions.

The effect of silence is magnified on the telephone. It's appropriate to be silent to listen, think, react, and allow what the other person has said to register. Silence allows the other person to finish a thought and be complete. Being silent allows the other person room to expound without the benefit of visual feedback, but don't overdo it.

Long silences on the telephone are perceived as hostile and withholding. The longest silence that can be tolerated without explanation is about ten seconds. Fifteen seconds produces doubt, and anxiety just builds after that. Remember, if your silence makes the other person anxious, you are being hurtful and creating resentment.

A Brief Course in Telephone Manners

Since you cannot tell how other people are feeling before you call, you need others' help. Your best allies are the people who work for the people you want to talk to. There are a lot of different ways of going about this but they all boil down to one simple thought.

Be nice to the little people.

Treating secretaries as equals often gets you further than

treating their bosses as equals. Make it a point to know the names of the assistants to the people you contact regularly. Their names should be written right below their bosses' in your telephone book. Spending a few pleasant moments with someone's secretary is always in your interest. Anyone who deals with important people will be quick to tell you how much they owe to their assistants.

Put yourself in the secretary's position. She wants to help her boss and protect him or her from harassment. She will hear complaints about any unnecessary or annoying calls she lets through. Let her help you with your problem.

If it's not a good time to call, ask her if she can suggest a better time. Find out when he is alone in the office and if he answers his own phone.

It's not a good idea to get into a pitch with a secretary. She's only empowered to discourage nuisances and going into a pitch reveals your desperation and can make you sound like a nuisance even if you aren't.

More properly stated, your desperation makes you into a nuisance.

Put a smile in your voice. It shows. It's important.

WHEN YOU GET THROUGH

When you reach your party, even if you've been cleared, you should ask again if this is a good time for him to talk. Give the other person a choice. He'll appreciate it and respect you for it because you are obviously treating him the way you want to be treated. You risk little by being courteous. Setting the tone for an honest, unpressured conversation always works in your favor. You want the best possible atmosphere for your conversation. If the atmosphere isn't important, the call probably isn't either and shouldn't have been made.

The way people answer your phone is you. So when others

answer the phone for you, give them specific instructions about how you want to be represented. The person who answers your phone is your spokesperson, the first contact a stranger has with you or your organization. Others form an opinion of you the moment they respond. Think about the impression you want to make and ask yourself if your person creates it.

The people who answer the phone for an enterprising company should project accessibility and positiveness. Their tone of voice should convey the following messages:

I'm glad you called.

I have the time to understand what you want.

We can solve it.

I'm sure we can find a way to work together.

You matter.

Your business is important.

This is a good place to work.

We like people.

This attitude should be a true reflection of what others can expect dealing with you or your company.

Negative people do not belong on the telephone.

Putting people on hold is an insult. It's made worse by not telling them first, and it is made intolerable by forcing them to listen to an arrangement of "Moon River" that sounds as if it was copied from some airline's in-flight music package. Putting someone on hold obligates them to listen. Silence at least lets them think. If you have a musical-hold option, resist using it.

Never put someone on hold for longer than one minute. When you are on hold, by thirty seconds negative feelings start to build. By forty-five seconds you begin to ask, "Where the hell is he?" When you are on hold, you are trapped on the phone, because if you hang up, even after ten minutes, others will know who you are and you run the risk of creating a negative impression.

Putting someone on hold makes them a prisoner, builds resentment, and undermines goodwill. Have the other person call back or call them back. But if you say you will call back in five minutes, be sure you do. If someone puts you on hold for a long time, hang up and call back immediately saying you were cut off, and make other arrangements for the call. If you must put a person on hold, have someone get back to them periodically. I can't think of a good thing to say about being on hold.

THE TELEPHONE CALL AS BUSINESS MEETING

A telephone call needs as much organization and planning as any other business meeting. Because everyone tends to become absorbed in their own needs, it's easy to forget about the other person's pressures and be intrusive. Avoid calling people casually unless you have a personal relationship. The unstructured telephone call is unwise. It dilutes your effectiveness and positions you as needy or annoying.

Treat all your business calls seriously.

Again, always call with specific goals in mind.

Ask yourself the following questions: Why am I calling? What do I hope to accomplish? What do I want to know? Will this telephone call give me that answer? Is there any other way I can find out? How can this call hurt me? What can I do to prevent that?

SETTING LIMITS

Limit the conversation. Keep it eventful. If you let it drift, it will lose its effectiveness. Don't try to discuss everything in a single call. It gets confusing. Stay focused. The other person should be able to report your message in a single sentence.

Don't bring up subjects that you are unprepared to discuss.

If the other person brings up a point that you don't want to discuss, postpone the discussion. Say you don't have time or would prefer to discuss it in person. Don't even begin to comment on the points. Don't get angry if the other person presses. Be polite but firm.

Some of the worst business mistakes have occurred because someone got into a discussion against his will or when he was unprepared to face an issue. Don't get trapped into this.

It's good business to expect to succeed.

WHEN PEOPLE WON'T TAKE YOUR CALLS

People avoid you because they don't want to face the problem that comes with you. When you become identified with a problem or are seen one-dimensionally as the critical boss, the whining parent, the pleading child, or the overbearing associate, you will be treated in a stereotyped way. You will be dealing with conditioned resistance. Salesmen face this problem in every call, meeting people who are prepared to say no.

To break the pattern, people often try to adopt a ploy or find some gimmick, but these approaches miss the point. People resent people who are trying to use or trick them. Gimmicks are risky and usually backfire. They are only good if you play percentages, not when every call matters.

You present yourself as an ally by being an ally. That is the best way to be sure others take your calls.

One of the best salesmen I know often spends hours on a call without making a sale. He services the account, takes an inventory, measures progress, evaluates his products' acceptance, and examines clients' complaints. His telephone calls are never refused because he is seen as part of the team, not an outsider.

Sincerity is the best gimmick for being accepted.

HARASSING CALLS

If you want to avoid harassing calls, take the call and be direct. Indicate that you don't want to talk to the caller, that because he or she is so difficult you have given your business to someone else, and that you will not take future calls. This will shut off most callers. It is amazing how many people waste time dodging unwanted calls without ever bringing the issue to a head.

Weed out everything in your life that keeps you from thriving.

WHEN YOU SHOULDN'T CALL

Never express anger over the phone. You can't tell how it is being received. It's precarious enough to express anger in a business situation without increasing your jeopardy by dealing in the dark. Expressing anger will always work against you. It's better to wait for another day when passions have subsided and you can express your disappointment calmly. Even so, you should consider the impact that getting emotional will have on your business relationships, credibility, and work atmosphere. And decide against it.

On the other hand, the integrity of a personal relationship depends on expressing your feelings as soon as they occur, but even then it is advisable to do this in person.

To develop an effective telephone style, be your best, your most natural self. Know what you want. Keep introductions short and get to the point as soon as possible.

Remember, the best calls state and answer a single question clearly. So don't waste time. Your directness identifies you as a serious business person.

Avoid putting pressure on the other person. It's just as easy for them to cut you off as it is for you to pressure them.

ANSWERING MACHINES

Whenever you place a call, you should be prepared to leave a message on an answering machine.

Keep it simple. Don't get cute.

If you reach a machine and don't want to leave a message, hang up immediately. If you have any hesitation, give only your name and number.

Don't leave a message if this is your first contact. If you make a mistake, it will be on tape and you will only feel inhibited about calling back. Don't add to your risk unnecessarily.

YOUR ANSWERING MACHINE

The right message for your answering machine conveys your style with confidence. The more confident you are, the less you need to say. This is not accomplished by hiring a firm to record your message. Adding music or other production value to your answering machine message is always a distraction. It's fine if on your personal line you want to tell jokes, or have the latest rock hit in the background. It may try the patience of your friends who will probably forgive your self-indulgence, but it's acceptable. It is entirely out of place in business.

The simplest and shortest message is the best.

"Hello. This is Bill Smith. Please leave your name and number and any message you like. I'll return your call as soon as I can." If this isn't personal enough for you, you should have an answering service, not a more clever message.

HANGING UP

Never hang up in anger.

Practice hanging up with a smile on your face and a thank-you. Indicate that you are glad to have spoken together. Take the essence of the call and translate it into a direction. Finally, close with a statement like "We'll get right to work on that," or "You'll hear from me in a week." That transforms the call into action.

Think about your use of the telephone. It deserves your fullest attention.

Chapter Six _____

WRITTEN COMMUNICATION

_____

Letters

You don't have to be a great writer to write effectively. You just have to be clear about what you want and state it directly. If you have difficulty putting your ideas into words, your problem lies here.

You are not clear when you fear being rejected. You hide your intentions when you fear being tested.

You cannot be clear expressing ideas to others if you aren't clear about them yourself. The belief that you are clear, but have a problem expressing yourself, is a self-deception. If you're not clear, you either don't understand what you are talking about or fear examining your own position.

If you aren't clear, you don't want to face a risk.

If you aren't clear, you probably haven't thought your idea through. Perhaps you only have half an idea. That's fine; just recognize it as such. The best ideas, the ones that have really reshaped the world, were once only incomplete notions, elusive suggestions that something could be. Ideas develop as you seek to complete them. In other words, when you try to be clear about them.

Becoming clear about your intention is the essence of all direct communication and especially of good writing. The other person wants to know what you mean and what you want. Your communication should answer those questions.

Anything less than an open, honest, and clearly written letter is a failure in communication.

THE LETTERS THAT NO ONE BOTHERS TO READ

Letters like the following are common to mass mailings.

Try to disguise the fact that they are selling something.

Offer to give something away for nothing.

Ask for a few minutes of your time.

Make outlandish promises.

Are obviously computer-generated, address you by your first name, and try to sound chummy.

Tell you that you have been chosen for some honor or special privilege, but only if you act now.

Pose a question you could not possibly respond to negatively, such as "How would you like to win $250,000 cash, a villa on the Riviera, or a new sports car?"

Such letters are considered successful if they achieve a four-percent response. Too many businesspeople rely on these mass-mailing approaches in their business correspondence and put people off unnecessarily. You cannot afford to create the wrong impression. Your correspondence must be one hundred percent effective.

KEEPING YOUR LETTER OUT OF THE WASTEBASKET

Most of the advice offered below is common sense and should be followed in all business communication, but because of the permanence of the written word it is especially important to bear in mind when writing letters. Imagine what would happen if your letter were photocopied and circulated. If you make a big enough fool of yourself it might be.

Don't get cute.

Don't boast, brag, or search for compliments.

Don't show off. The effect wears thin on a second reading.

Don't use a big vocabulary, either general or technical. Sesquipedalianism obfuscates pellucidity. If you get my drift.

Don't make blind assumptions about what the reader wants or needs. If you're wrong, you lose all your credibility.

Don't write a legalistic letter in the hopes of convincing someone of your position.

Don't use nicknames unless you are on those terms with the other person. Don't be familiar. Don't make reference to personal matters in the other person's life. Don't send regards to people you have never met except at Christmas.

Don't be insincere.

Don't complain.

Don't undermine.

WHAT YOU SHOULD NEVER PUT INTO WRITING

Never use a letter to set someone up.

Never threaten. Threatening to apply pressure, take punitive action, or seek sanctions can and will work against you. Just indicate that you want to avoid unnecessary problems and resolve differences agreeably. Pointing out dire consequences to frighten the other party to get them to act the way you want is a manipulation. If you feel you have to take intimidating action, do so face to face, not in writing. Threatening is a negotiating tactic, and a questionable one at that. It creates anxiety and you need to be in the other person's presence to make it work for you. Otherwise if the other person takes your threatening letter seriously, he only hardens in his position and makes resolution more difficult. If he doesn't take it seriously, you only look foolish.

Never let off steam in a business letter. While venting anger in a personal letter is useful, it violates good business practice.

Never put someone down. If you have a criticism, make it in person so you can prepare the other person and study his or her reaction. Criticizing puts people on the defensive, closing them off to new ideas. Criticizing people in a letter, because of the physical distance between parties only increases isolation and negativity.

Never criticize another person's company, employees, tactics, judgment, policy, or attitude. Consider how he would react to such a comment. What is his alternative, but to react negatively. If you have helpful suggestions to make, do so when asked to or when the suggestion can be heard and implemented.

Never send a letter without a clear purpose.

Never lead someone on.

THE EFFECTIVE BUSINESS LETTER

Assume a favorable result.

Before you write a letter, remind yourself of your long-term goals. Assume that the best possible situation will eventually result and make your letter a step toward that desired success. Reflect this positive attitude throughout your letter, especially the difficult sections. Point out problems with confidence since your intention is to resolve them. Do not use them to break the business relationship. Imagine for a moment that several years have passed and you have accomplished your goals. Borrow optimism from that future viewpoint and indicate what you should do to correct the present situation.

That is your letter. Put it down.

How you convey your intention depends on who you are writing to and what their needs are, but you must always be true to your own style and taste. Everyone who writes effective letters projects a good sense of him or herself.

When you think, you hear a voice speaking in your head. Try to write in that voice without adding to it. The flow you seek to capture in your writing is your natural progression from thought to thought. Put it all down as it comes to you. Trust yourself. Don't judge. Edit later.

THE ONE-PAGE RULE

A business letter longer than one page is unnecessary. It only reflects your disorganization. A long, involved letter indicates that you don't think well enough of your ideas to make them precise and understandable. Take the time to make your letters short.

A long letter means you do not value your reader's time. It means you don't know what you want. It says you are too unsure to come directly to the point.

A one-page letter gives your reader power, to grasp, accept or reject. It says you respect your reader's decision-making power by presenting the facts clearly. It shows that you believe in yourself.

FORM FOR THE CORRECT BUSINESS LETTER

Salutation

Keep it simple. Avoid being familiar.

Opening Paragraph
State the purpose of the letter in a single sentence.
>Make a statement and indicate the reasons for your belief.
>State the facts clearly and without slanting them.
>Interpret these facts briefly if necessary.

Paragraph Two
State your position.
>Make your offer.
>Summarize your expectations to work together profitably.

Closing
Reflect your positive attitude.

If you can't see a profitable outcome in doing business with the other person, you shouldn't write the letter.

If you are saying no to someone else's proposal, do so in the first sentence and close. Be respectful. If you think you might like to do business with this person at some future time, be sure you indicate that you are receptive to further discussions. Remember, this may be the only opportunity you'll have to do business together. If you don't want to do business, thank the other person for his interest, but indicate clearly that you have no opportunity for doing business with him at this time.

The correct business letter is simple and direct. It states its message at the outset.

AN ATTITUDE CHECK

After you finish the letter, read it. Does it convey what you intended? Is there any way the reader might confuse your meaning?

Consider how that person will react. Is there any other way that one could react?

What is the attitude of the person writing the letter? Is it sincere, pushy, selling, desperate, angry, uncertain, or vague?

What impression does it make on you? Would you be encouraged to do business with this person?

Is the letter too personal, too stiff, too tentative, or too rigid?

Can you summarize the letter in a single sentence? Is that sentence in the letter? Or better yet, should that sentence be the letter?

Is there anything about your letter that could put someone off?

If you received this letter, when would you stop reading? Why is it longer than that?

How would you respond to this letter?

THE LETTERS NO ONE CAN OVERLOOK—THE SINGLE-SENTENCE LETTER

Designing your letter as a telegram is wonderfully effective if you know precisely what you want and are sure of yourself. The one-sentence letter is intensely personal and reveals even more about you than a longer letter. It can be a powerful statement of your confidence, but you risk having it backfire. Because you have to expose yourself in a single sentence without introduction, exposition, explanation, qualification, or second chance, you are much more vulnerable and can be misunderstood. You also risk overpowering a less secure person who may feel the need to put you down and not take you seriously.

The single-word letter is even more effective, has even greater impact, and is even riskier. Quotable and provocative, it requires creativity and brimming self-confidence. A good example is General Patton's response when asked to surrender. "Nuts," he said. But always think of the person receiving the letter and measure the effect of the impact.

Remember, you write to get results. Ask yourself if your letter will achieve the results you want. If it won't, don't send it.

99

LETTERS OTHER PEOPLE WANT TO READ

Good news.
  Praise.
  Positive feedback.
  Confirmation of the rightness of their decision or policy.

THE FRAMABLE LETTER

You have great power to validate others merely by writing a letter expressing your appreciation. Giving positive feedback reassures people that someone notices them and values their contribution. Receiving a letter like this can be an important event in another person's life.

If you decide to write such a letter, avoid using the pronoun "I." The subject of this letter is not intended as flattery or to win esteem for you, but to give sincere recognition. If you think the other person will be suspicious, begin with a brief explanation. Tell how long you've been thinking about writing and how deserved your praise is.

Keep it brief and unembarrassing. Receiving it should make the other person proud, happy, and enjoy sharing it with someone else.

THE SELF-SERVING LETTER

The self-serving letter is usually written at a time of conflict between you and the recipient. It attempts to create evidence by setting forth your viewpoint of the dispute as if it represents the true facts. It does not try to be evenhanded. It is written with the hope that the recipient will show it to his lawyer who will then discourage him from taking action unfavorable to you. Therefore, it states the facts as you see them and, by prejudicially relating how the other person presented himself, justifies your actions. The self-serving letter defines a context. Quoting the other person, referring to critical documents and events, establishing the correctness of your argument and the thin grounds of the other person's reasoning, are its essence. It puts people on notice. It states your willingness to stand up for your rights and to take action. It is meant to intimidate the other person. It does not invite debate and is a way of calling the other person's bluff. It is often one small step removed from litigation.

The Memo

The best way to think of a memo is as a directive in another person's life.

"Call on Smith first. If he accepts, use it to sell Jones."

"Don't respond if he asks. Just say you don't know."

Some of the best memos comment on job performance. Think of them as a grade if you like. They should always be brief. They should always be necessary. They should extend your influence by carrying forth your attitude and intention.

EXAMPLES OF EFFECTIVE MEMOS

"Great!"

"I agree."

"Present this to the chief yourself. It's wonderful and you deserve the credit."

"Are your figures mistaken on items 4 and 5?"

"Too long."

"Good direction. . . . See me about this."

"More . . ."

"Fix section on inventory. Otherwise fine."

A single question makes an ideal memo, especially when attached to an article or document.

"Sell? Hold? Buy more?"

"Should we be involved in this?"

"Do you think the competition knows about this?"

A memo should be as private as a personal letter. It is an intimate comment that shapes another's actions. It is a spur, a form of feedback. A good memo is also a reward and can lift the spirits of the receiver and increase productivity.

The memo is a simple and effective way to bolster someone's pride. It is a direct and informal form of communication whose impact is often underestimated. It takes only a moment to send a memo.

Send a memo when you feel good about someone's work. Sharing your feelings builds confidence and loyalty. It provides immediate gratification and offers positive reinforcement. Most important, it makes a habit of expressing appreciation.

Counterproductive memos are negative intrusions in the working day. They criticize, nag, go on for two and three and four pages that no one wants or bothers to read, and leave the receiver feeling defeated, like quitting, demoralized, inferior, or found out again.

If you have an important criticism to make, a memo is not the right place to express yourself. Try meeting face to face with the other person. When you write a negative memo, you usually hurt the other person.

Counterproductive memos demand replies, additional reports, long explanations, and follow-ups. In short, they waste time and money, and undermine confidence and enthusiasm.

Negative memos are almost always the product of a controlling, self-important, rigid person who is out of touch with the people who work with or for him and who is uncomfortable dealing with people directly.

Everyone who works with this person knows this except the person in question.

People like this use memos as a form of punishment. They see the memo as instruction, but really use it to force their way on others. They never take the time to think how the person receiving their memo will feel. Almost always their memos create more stress and do not move the problem any closer to solution.

You can include negative comments in a memo if you do so with a positive attitude that conveys hopefulness, a belief in the other person, and a direction that will resolve the difficulty.

If you must write a negative memo just to get the negativity out of your system, do so, but don't send it.

If you value your ideas, take time to be clear about sharing them and design your written work to bring you closer to your goals.

Chapter Seven _____

HOW TO RUN A BUSINESS MEETING

_____

The Formal Business Meeting

Everyone in business spends time in business meetings. When people schedule time to share ideas, discuss problems, progress, or planning, they are having a formal business meeting even though only two people may be involved and it lasts only a few minutes.

A good business meeting clarifies directions, creates plans, sets priorities, delegates responsibility, allows for participation, and enhances a sense of cohesion and unity.

People dislike business meetings for good reasons. Most business meetings are a waste of time; they are poorly planned and administered, and provide an arena more for the display of egos, competitiveness, and power than for work. Most business meetings could be profitably eliminated.

Much of this wastefulness is derived from the business meeting's uneventful nature. In regularly scheduled meetings, most of what is discussed is catch-up material, minutes of the last meeting, filler, and so on. In time people begin to resent such meetings and see them as repetitive, or uncreative, or distracting from real work. Some of the people who flourish in the meeting environment are not particularly motivated workers who are glad for a recess. They see meetings as a social event. They participate gladly and the real workers make fun of them. A good reason for keeping the workers and those who talk about the work apart.

Having meetings just for the sake of having meetings is operating at the lowest level of efficiency. Meetings need the thrust of reality to keep them focused. The best are problem-oriented. The worst are pointless discussions.

Getting "Up" for the Meeting

All business meetings require preparation. The object of the meeting is to solve a problem and move forward. What happens in a meeting is a direct reflection of the leader's energy and organization, so you should have a clear idea of what you want to accomplish. You should anticipate the problems people will have dealing with your point of view and have some notion of who will object and to what. To be an effective group leader, don't permit your comfort or effectiveness to depend on what anyone else in the group says or feels. Be above this. You are a facilitator. You need to be disinterested, motivated to define and solve a problem, and satisfied that others are willing to contribute their best effort. Encourage others to present their views by giving them an open forum to make their point.

You need to get up for the meeting.

Even if you take only a few minutes to do so, prepare yourself. Consider what you want to accomplish. How necessary is the meeting? If you cannot convince yourself that the meeting is important, it is unlikely that you are going to convince anyone else. Picture the meeting in your mind. Imagine the scenes you would like to take place. Set your determination to have a productive and constructive meeting.

Write out the purpose of the meeting in a single sentence. The clearer you are on this, the more likely you are to accomplish your objectives. If you are unclear, the meeting will drift aimlessly and you will tend to focus impulsively on the points that others bring up merely because they seem to give direction or ground you. Your uncertainty also creates restlessness. You lose others' attention and undermine your credibility as a leader. Your aimlessness also offers an opening for manipulative types who will flatter you and second your vague ideas, pronouncing them "wonderful" as they lead you astray. You can't lead if you depend on other people's support for your leadership.

On the other hand, don't be fixed in your belief about what you want to take place. If you are that sure of what you want, why not save everyone the time and effort and simply issue a statement? People resent a leader insincerely seeming to be democratic more than they do a leader who asserts himself dictatorially.

The next step is to design the meeting.

Consider where you want the meeting to take place. If you are a superior, inviting one other person to your office reasserts your power and authority. When you design a meeting you should make the surroundings work for your subject. It's sometimes helpful to have a meeting in the other person's work space. It's familiar and offers an opportunity to study his environment. Is it productive? How often is he interrupted? Does he isolate himself? Could you function here? How does it feel being here?

Tell others beforehand what you plan to discuss. Invite them to create their own agenda. Limit their anxiety by stressing the positive aspects of your meeting. By focusing on your general goal, you free others to think about a problem rather than spur them on to ruminate obsessively about what they may have done wrong. This is especially important when you deal with a controlling person. Just thinking that another person is going to judge him or her can preoccupy a controlling person for days.

Some Practical Advice for the Group Leader

The function of the leader is to direct the group so that at the end of the meeting everyone feels it was important to have been there, that he had an effect on the outcome, that his contribution mattered, and that his opinion was heard.

The leader is not the center of the group, but its catalyst. The best way for the leader to use his power is to identify and follow the most promising direction without dominating. Participants shouldn't have to ask for the leader's approval to speak. If the leader is in control, he need only smile to get someone to speak or look over at an intrusive questioner to silence him.

Be as subtle and as light-handed as possible. Once you have stated your question, ask for a consensus to see what other people think about the problem. Ask, "Is this the right question?" "Do any of you have an opinion of how this meeting should proceed?" This invites others to relate to their agendas.

Pay attention to what is happening in the group.

Jealousies often appear as reflex disagreements, putdowns, or undermining. When a jealous person intrudes, ask him or her to make a positive suggestion.

Questions to Focus the Group

It's not necessary to have all the answers to be an effective leader. You just need to believe that there is an answer to the problem and that the group can come to it. Don't get trapped into believing you have to come up with inspiration that synthesizes all the information into a brilliant answer. Still, if a solution develops in a meeting you are leading, your leadership showed the way and you should be proud. That is what good leadership is all about. Actually, you don't need to know anything about the subject under discussion, but you need to be able to understand the inner workings of the group. Any group can and will respond to general directives. Remember, everyone is trying to be their best and show what they can do. If you give others a chance and are appreciative, they'll define and solve the problem for you.

"How else can we solve this problem?"

"What are the alternatives?"

These questions are useful because they encourage others to be creative. Field all responses receptively. Remember, your goal is to get others to contribute. If people do that, you are being effective.

"I don't understand."

"How does this work?"

These are especially useful comments because they encourage people to restate their logic, which reopens a particular topic for discussion. Remember, your failure to understand is not caused by your lack of intelligence but by the other person's vagueness. Ask others to become clearer. Let them help you understand.

"Where are we now?"

"Is this the right direction?"

When the discussion seems to repeat, or get lost, invite others to define where matters stand. After one or two people have commented, summarize by picking the direction you want the group to follow.

"What are we missing?"

"How could this go wrong?"

These questions help the group complete the idea and look at the risks.

When others play it safe and are unwilling to comment, pressuring them to contribute is self-defeating. Keep in mind that there are wide variations in personal style. If you anticipated the meeting correctly, you'll have a good idea of who will contribute and why. Prepare questions for silent types that reveal their strength and help them contribute. But don't make it an inquisition. Just have the questions in mind for the right opportunity. When the group as a whole doesn't respond, asking "How shall I interpret this silence?" provides an opening.

Reserve "Wonderful" and "Terrific" for comments when your meaning is at least "good." You need to have some consistency in your use of language. Hyping everyone up with lavish praise produces an insincere atmosphere and an abandonment of critical standards. In any case, praise the idea and direction rather than its author. That encourages others to contribute.

When the group succeeds and praises itself, don't discourage it. Whether it is winning a ball game, a military battle, or solving a marketing problem, the positive group spirit that emanates from winning is also the group's reward. The danger comes when the group overly praises accomplishments that no one outside the group would even value. This self-generated enthusiasm only dilutes genuine positive feelings. When everyone feels wonderful about everything all the time, no one feels really good about anything.

Encourage your group to feel good about real accomplishments and demonstrate your wariness when members seem to be getting unrealistic. Challenge them with a statement like "Yes, it's a great plan, but will it really work? What could go wrong?" This is not deflating their egos but using their good feeling as leverage to investigate the downside risk. It's always more profitable to look at the negative side of a situation when you are feeling good. The openness you bring to a situation when you feel undefended can help solve problems no one wanted to admit even existed before.

As a leader you should always be a little removed from the emotions of the group. This allows you to make observations about the group's progress.

As a leader the best way to make your own points is to discover your ideas and conclusions in others' comments and give them the credit. Draw your ideas out of them by introducing your points with comments like "You mean . . . ," "Are you really saying . . . ," and "Do I have this correct . . . ?" This gives the other person credit, brings your point to the surface, and yet keeps you out of the discussion. It's best, of course, if the entire group gets credit for the idea.

Having someone make the comment you want by prior arrangement is always a bad maneuver. No matter what you think, everyone will know you were behind it and your meeting will look like the set-up affair it is. If your idea is good, it will evolve through your careful listening and support. If it doesn't, you can always suggest it as an alternative for discussion later on.

If you make a suggestion and the group rejects it, don't get heavy-handed. Try to understand their resistance and allow it to come to the surface without threatening or implying punitive action. You want their honest appraisal, so be good-humored and accepting.

If the members of the group refer to themselves as "we" and to the project as "ours," you are running the meeting properly.

Chapter Eight _____

HOW TO
INTERVIEW

Success depends as much on the information you receive as it does on your ability to analyze it. The purpose of interviewing is to discover people's strengths and weaknesses, so you can help them make the most of themselves and keep them out of trouble. Effective interviewers trust their instincts.

Before you interview someone be sure you know what you are looking for; otherwise you risk having the right person sit in front of you and not recognizing it. It's useful to make a list describing the features of the ideal applicant and put them in order of importance. Organize and direct your questioning. You'll be able to cut through extraneous material quickly and get to the heart of the matter. As a result you will make clearer, more certain judgments.

The interview begins the moment the other person walks through the door. Pay attention to your first impression. Always ask yourself how you feel in the other person's presence. Also ask why you feel what you feel. Do this continually during the interview. This inner awareness is the most important part of the interview.

Look at the other person's appearance. Put yourself in his place and ask what he had in mind when he dressed that morning. Consider his sense of style. Does he feel comfortable with it or is he trying to make an impression as something he is not? Is this person reaching or is he understated? The dress and behavior codes of some businesses are so unrealistic they undermine the purpose for which they were intended. Overly rigid standards don't protect against hiring losers or make it easier to find good people. The company always loses when blind enforcement of standards takes the place of thoughtful evaluation. Many misjudgments are made that could easily have been avoided if the interviewer had paid closer attention to his or her intuition.

The standards you employ should be appropriate to the position you seek to fill. If you are hiring someone to represent your company and project its image, every aspect of his appearance is important, including taste in clothes, firmness and dryness of handshake, confidence projected and tone of voice. While if you are looking for a computer programmer, a wrinkled shirt, torn sneakers and faded corduroy pants, and glasses that slip onto the nose don't matter at all. A lot of costly mistakes have been made by losing sight of priorities.

The best way to open an interview is to ask a question that reflects your interest in the points on your list. Let your desire to understand shape your questioning.

Allow the other person to talk. Avoid dominating the interview or setting rigid goals. Let it be the other person's interview. Be a thinking instrument. Be patient. Take your time to discover the other person.

If the other person says something that interests you, follow up by asking the questions that naturally occur to you. If you hear a discrepancy, ask for an explanation. Ask the other person why he believes what he does. Try to get an idea of the other person's thinking. If you are confused, invite the other person to make matters clear. Remember, you aren't supposed to know anything about the other person, so ask until you are satisfied. Does the person answer openly and spontaneously or does he insist on qualifying his answers? Is he able to give a frank opinion or does he avoid exposing himself? The way a person responds to questions also defines the way he takes risks. Be forgiving if he makes a slip. The ability to recognize mistakes and correct them is more valuable than giving a perfect but shallow impression.

The best way to make people comfortable is to respond positively every time they do well. Remember, you are trying to see how the other person functions at his best. Some people don't function well under stress and any interview situation unnerves them. With such people, it's useful to bring up strengths in their résumé or letters of recommendation. Helping the person you interview put his best foot forward will bring you far more information than pointing out his weaknesses. You can ask him about those later.

Here are some simple techniques for making people comfortable.

Look for something about the other person you like and mention it.

Smile.

Make positive comments like "Yes," "Good," "Exactly," "Of course," "I see," and "I agree," and act positively. Nod agreement. Be appreciative, sincere, and listen.

Once the other person starts to talk, let him. Don't worry about his getting lost or wasting time. You are trying to establish a flow of ideas. You can be an active listener merely by thinking, "Yes." Once you have established yourself as a supportive listener, it will be easy to lead the discussion wherever you choose. The best audience gets the best performance.

Creating stress to see how applicants function under pressure is manipulative and risky. It puts others at a disadvantage and invites them to perform at their worst. It is generally counterproductive and should be avoided.

Nonetheless, it is useful to confront them when you suspect that other people are not being honest or frank about their faults. Be direct about this. If the other person argues with you, explain that you have difficulty understanding and would like to know more. How they respond to your invitation to be forthright tells you what you should know about them.

When a difficulty arises in an interview, it can be put to your advantage. If the other person reacts peculiarly, try to define what happened and why it was so disturbing. People always try to protect themselves in stressful situations. Finding out why reveals their character.

Although it's natural to try to avoid conflict, should conflict occur, use it to discover something about the other person. Ask, "What just happened here?" Describe what you observed and then ask, "What is your view of the situation?" Now observe how your interviewee responds. Does he deny that a problem exists? Does he get sullen or withdrawn, or act as if he's been uncovered? Does he seem blocked. If the other person welcomes the opportunity and works with you, you've discovered a valuable worker.

Give others permission to bring up their discontent. You need to learn to feel comfortable encouraging others to express negative feelings. Since resentment is withheld hurt, helping others express their disappointment always opens up the interview. It may get a bit heated, but if you don't take it personally it will pass. Difficult interview situations are made far worse when the interviewer tries to keep painful matters hidden.

Evaluating Your Interview Experience

If credentials were all that mattered, the interview would be unnecessary, but everyone knows of people who have impeccable work qualifications and dreadful interpersonal skills. The interview is the instrument that evaluates what cannot be gleaned from a résumé or letters of recommendation. Don't be swayed by an impressive background. See that background as the ticket for admission to the interview and give the interview independent status.

Consider how this person makes you feel. Do you like being with him or her? What contribution do you think this person would make to the mood of the people around him? Ask yourself what it would be like to work with this person on a daily basis. Would you find it depressing, inspiring, boring, a drain, or a privilege? What is the feeling the other person projects, optimism or defeat?

Is this person really interested in his work? Does he have a strong sense of industry? Will he enhance the productivity of the workplace?

Would you feel comfortable going to lunch with this person? Is he socially aware, poised, and confident? Do you feel any embarrassment for him or being with him? If you do, be certain that placing such a person with insecure people who are easily embarrassed by the company they keep will create problems.

More important than raw credentials is attitude. A person who criticizes others is unlikely to be supportive when things go wrong. A person who does his best work has little reason to criticize others. He simply assumes that they are doing their best as well.

Happy people don't look for trouble.

How open is the other person? How freely does he bring up subjects, comment on articles in the office, or ask questions? Are his questions pertinent? Do they represent a deep thought process or a superficial, perhaps anxiety-driven flightiness? How much does he talk about hardship and doom? People who continually point out the dismal side of situations may be playing devil's advocate, or may just be negative people; but some of these people are depressed.

How loyal is this person? Can you count on him? How do

you know? How does he speak of other people? Is he fair, generous, or bitter? Whom does he regard as his friend? Whom does he see as betraying him?

How hard does the person try to impress you? You get a good idea of a person's values by his attempt to convince you of his worth. Imagine yourself as the narrator of his history. Would you have brought out the points he did? What does his emphasis tell you? What points does he repeat? Is there a pattern? What does it mean? People who struggle to impress you reveal their insecurity about the very things they brag about, and show their lack of insight into themselves. They think you can't tell.

Pay attention to the other person's presentation. He's thought about what he was going to say and how he would say it, so his comments reflect what he thinks is important.

More important than anything on the résumé is the way the résumé is discussed. A professional résumé is often so sterilized that it tells very little about the person. Notice if the résumé avoids the truth or tries to disguise the facts. You are trying to distill a total sense of the person, not merely identify a point or two you can use to support a quick judgment. However, if you just don't like the person and are open about your reasons, that is a valid appraisal. While if you are attracted to someone no one else likes, that is also valid. It may be the special chemistry with you that gives someone the big break he's been waiting for. You can make great discoveries in people. Wonderful people can get lost in large companies, talents can be overlooked, and for lack of someone's belief and encouragement, perfectly good people become disillusioned and give up.

Don't be afraid to believe in someone. The object of a good interview is to assess a person's capacity for growth. A person with high potential likes to work, works hard, and is eager to get started. He is open, especially about failures, and yet has a sense of pride, achievement, and delight in his successes. He doesn't give up. He is honest, asks questions freely, and admits what he doesn't know. He admits unflattering criticism without excuses and accepts blame without long explanations. He makes helpful contributions without asking for credit and willingly shares the glory. He is interested in others and has a sense of humor about himself.

Value the good you discover in others and comment on it favorably when you do. You'll be amazed at how much more people will reveal to you.

At some point you need to give the other person an honest appraisal of what you have found, what you think of him, and what his chances are. Be honest, but be kind. If you're not able to hire him, don't push him out just to get him out of your way. There's no point in adding to someone's hopelessness. If you have genuine positive feelings about this person, take time to share them. If you have other leads or suggestions, be generous with them. The word to remember at this time is "give."

You've held a unique advantage over this person for the past few minutes and now have a special viewpoint that could be helpful to him. It is a precious moment for you. If you can add something positive to this person's life, do so. You have an opportunity to do some good just by being yourself. If you are giving of yourself, this moment can be the most rewarding and meaningful of your day.

It can make your job.

In order for the interview to have lasting value, it must be a valid reflection of the company behind it. It must have integrity, sincerity, and honesty. Otherwise it is only a time-consuming game and a sad one at that.

Chapter Nine _____

HOW TO TAKE
AN INTERVIEW

_____

The best way to approach an interview is with the belief that if the situation is right for you, it is going to turn out right, and if it's not, it won't. This may sound fatalistic, but it's the truth. Learning interviewing techniques can give you more confidence and even show you how to turn a hostile interview around and make it work for you, but the best psychological approach is to be yourself. If you have to be so on your toes during an interview that you cannot be yourself, the chances are you are applying at the wrong place.

Consider if the situation you are applying for is really in your interest instead of focusing on how to manipulate the interview. If your chief concern is to comply with someone else's standards, you risk losing your direction and, therefore, your greatest chances for advancement and success. If you view the interview as trying to convince someone to employ you, all you are looking for is a job. A job is only a job. Even if you haven't found it, your life has a broader purpose. This purpose needs to be expressed as your lifework and the position you are seeking should help you discover or fulfill your potential by providing an opportunity to grow. If it doesn't, years from now you'll end up with a résumé that is no more than a list of jobs that went nowhere.

The most important part of your résumé is the growth it reveals. Did you learn your lessons and move ahead or did you become trapped in situations out of a lack of belief in yourself? Of course loyalty, consistency, and reliability are important to a company when they hire you, but when times are difficult and it comes down to laying people off, you'll discover to your bitterness and disillusionment that loyalty is not nearly as important as the ability to adapt and solve problems. Your best protection is to take a position where you can grow more valuable and to approach the interview looking for the opportunity that is best for you.

When workers feel their company prevents them from contributing their ideas and as they observe their superiors making mistakes that they could have prevented, they lose respect for the organization and for themselves for being there. When individual contribution is not encouraged, productivity always suffers. Since the company you are applying to is going to be looking out for itself, you have to look out for yourself. Seek work that allows you to develop your abilities. Whenever you feel confined in an interview or find the job description limiting, there is a strong likelihood that you won't be encouraged to grow, just expected to do the job.

The interview belongs as much to you as it does to the company interviewing you. Be selfish in assessing the position. Where will this job take you ten years from now? Is this an opportunity to progress on your own merits or a position on a slow-moving conveyor belt where advancement comes only by death and acts of God? You have to be willing to risk everything in the interview.

You display your highest intelligence when you openly express your natural curiosity. Trust that you have a good mind and share your thoughts. Make your point. Ask your question, but don't get emotionally attached to your ideas or insist that others agree.

Being flexible is far more valuable than being right or knowing all the facts. Accept that you're not perfect. The best defense against an overpowering interviewer is to disarm him or her with your openness.

Your shortcomings are not nearly as important as the way you deal with them. Interviewers are looking for people who are aware of their shortcomings, are open about admitting them, and ask for help when they need it. Since most of what goes wrong could have been caught and corrected earlier if people were open, a good interviewer will be more interested in what you learned from your failures than in the failures themselves. The correct attitude to project in an interview is that you are concerned with doing a good job, are eager to listen and learn, and are willing to do whatever needs to be done to get the job done. Demonstrating your flexibility without appearing spineless is the delicate balance you are trying to achieve.

The greatest pressure you'll feel in an interview won't come from the interviewer but from within yourself when you try to remain hidden. An interviewer is only as threatening as you are concealing. The stress of maintaining your cover-up gives you away. It only signals a good interviewer to press harder and discover what you are hiding.

To relieve such stress, share your thinking. Telling the interviewer what you were hesitant in revealing not only makes you feel better, it lowers his guard and takes the heat off his frontal attack. Interviewers love to get to the bottom of a mystery and will feel as if they are successful and that you are cooperative and friendly.

More important than the information you give is the way it is presented. So if you make an important mistake in the interview, don't ignore it even if the interviewer hasn't noticed. If you say something you don't mean, correct yourself. Saying, "That's not accurate, I meant to say . . ." is usually all that's needed. If the interviewer asks why you erred, just say you were concerned about making the best impression. This will enhance your credibility and relax you. There is nothing worse than getting in over your head and trying to cover up. It's almost always disastrous. The deeper you get, the more embarrassing it is for everyone and the more difficult it is to turn matters around. Unfortunately, this often happens in situations that are really important to you.

I had always wanted to go to Harvard. I had dozens of friends there, knew my way around campus, and dressed and acted the part. My grades, extracurricular activities, and letters of recommendation were excellent. I just needed to get through the interview. I stopped in a bookstore in Cambridge just before my interview and found a copy of Freud's *Psychopathology of Everyday Life*, just the thing to carry with me to make an additional statement, I thought, and was off to the interview. I opened the book in the waiting room and struggled though the opening pages where Freud was discussing the unconscious meaning of forgetting. Understandably, I was unable to concentrate and the theories Freud was discussing baffled me. I felt a bit stupid, to tell the truth, and I suddenly had doubts about myself. I tried to put the book away as I went into the interview, but the interviewer saw it and began the interview with the question, "So what do you think of Freud's theories?"

It was all downhill from that point as I tried to explain something I hadn't understood at all. Out of my insecurity I felt that because I had read ten pages, I had to understand perfectly. I gave an explanation so full of symbolic anxiety that Freud would have had a field day analyzing it. The interviewer was not amused and his displeasure precipitated further panic in me as I saw my dreams and hopes go down the drain. I got deeper and deeper in trouble. No escape. I could have saved myself just by telling the truth, but by then it seemed too overwhelming. Because I couldn't admit my humanness I came off as a phony. And I was.

Some interviewers are unfair. They are usually amateurs, directed by their own insecurity. There is nothing more vicious than frightened people with power. If you confront them, you risk retaliation. They cannot take criticism, especially about their abuse of power. It's just too close to home and makes them even more disagreeable.

When you realize that you are dealing with an unfair person, assume that the situation is probably lost and don't allow yourself to be dragged into his negativity. Such an interview is a fair warning of the way you would be treated if you were unlucky enough to be hired. If the boss is interviewing you, you can be certain that this is the case.

Should the interview go badly, don't ignore it. Prepare some questions to ask yourself that show your interest in the company and the position, and reveal your expertise. Your questions should be genuine to promote a flow of ideas. Phony questions go nowhere, seem out of place, and only draw attention to your awkwardness.

Don't be afraid to ask about the company's strength and future. Any hedging or qualifying should be a warning sign to you.

It's important to ask about opportunities for advancement. Spent years and expended energy cannot be reclaimed, so take advantage of this moment. It's far better to risk when you have the option of looking elsewhere than to enter into employment under false expectations only to be disappointed when promises aren't kept and you have too much invested to change.

After you have the information you want, ask the interviewer what he thought of the interview and what he thought of you. Summarize your impressions and your positive outlook and thank him for his time.

IV. Getting Results

Chapter Ten

INCREASING PRODUCTIVITY

The best and most lasting way to make people more productive is to identify with their needs and employ them for their strongest talents. Unfortunately, it is the rare worker who feels that he is doing what he wants and is being used to his fullest potential.

You can motivate people by manipulating them to perform, but this only ends up disheartening them. Getting people to do unpleasant jobs for more money only reminds them that they have a price and after a while even crass people begin to question their values. You can threaten workers and manage them by fear, but eventually people become accustomed to the threat and ignore you. People adapt to all stimuli so unless people are encouraged to motivate themselves all attempts at increasing productivity are short-lived.

When companies try to spur workers to higher productivity through external rewards, they run the risk of adaptive mechanisms eroding away the effectiveness of their efforts. After a while even greed fails as a motivator. To begin with, few companies can afford the kind of financial incentive that makes any real difference in the lives of their employees. Most financial rewards are quickly adjusted to. Although management seldom hears, workers often make fun of minor wage increases, cynically tallying the depreciating effect of inflation and taxes. Unless a worker's raise makes a noticeable change in life-style, it hardly serves as an incentive to produce and is viewed as expected and deserved, as purchasing power maintenance. The gratitude, enthusiasm, and increased productivity, if any, caused by a raise is short-lived. Attempting to motivate workers by external means requires ever-increasing external rewards to make the same impact. Eventually it becomes impractical to spend so much time motivating workers.

When an external reward is routinely expected, it no longer has a motivating impact.

However, the sudden threat of losing one's job has a powerful and often lasting effect in increasing productivity. The Chrysler Corporation's precarious position created a momentum that not only increased productivity and pulled the company out of danger, it created record profits years later. However, such incentives cannot be manufactured. They must be genuine. On the other hand, the chronic threat of losing one's job undermines self-esteem and always lowers productivity.

In most businesses, employees soon adapt to external incentives and become complacent as they find their own comfort levels. The key to increasing productivity is to tap into the individual's inner drives and identify with them. The best way to increase productivity is to see that people are doing jobs that they are most suited for and like best.

Using your own situation as an example, answer the following questions. This will help you evaluate your own productivity and understand what motivates you.

What do you do best?

How often do you do that?

What would you rather be doing than your present job?

Is there anyone with whom you would like to exchange jobs?

What appeals to you about the other job?

Can any part of this be included in your present work?

What stands in the way of you doing this?

What part of your job do you do least well?

How much of the time do you do this?

When are you most productive?

How often does this positive situation occur?

What does your productivity depend upon?

Are you able to "run" with your most productive times or does your schedule or other duties cut them short?

When are you happiest in your work?

Are these times the same as your productive times?

If you are doing what you are suited for, your happy times should be your most productive. What applies to you, applies to others.

Unfortunately, most businesses do not encourage workers to seek personal expression in their work. Production is isolated from pride. Personal satisfaction is not given as much importance as output. Some companies use only their employees' hands and waste their brains. Rather than trying to match the natural talent of a person with a job, people are used approximately and wear out. This is the main reason productivity falters.

People will work harder to grow than they will for an increase in salary. Even if it doesn't find expression, What's in it for me? is the question that is in every worker's heart. A higher salary may work less as an incentive and more as a drug if there is no real room for advancement or personal growth.

The way to encourage individual participation and tap individual resourcefulness is to ask for it. Everywhere you look in your company, good ideas are wasted simply because the people who have them feel inhibited about sharing them. They are afraid to speak up or that their advice isn't wanted. Companies send out for experts to tell them what's wrong and never ask the people who know first-hand. The first thing the experts do is interview the little people whom the company has been ignoring.

People want to be effective, to make a difference, to know that they contributed something of value. There is nothing so powerful, so uplifting, as knowing you really matter. Nor is anything so undermining or demoralizing as believing you can be replaced or are not taken seriously.

The greatest growth is achieved by people who find individual purpose in their work rather than those who see it as a financial means to some symbolic reward. The difference is in being content and loving what you do all the time compared to having a large disposable income, but being drained by the way you earn it.

If the price you pay for security weakens your self-esteem, you have no security at all. Real security shouldn't make you restless at night. It's hard to have peace of mind when you suspect your work is meaningless and that you are wasting your life.

Praise is a powerful motivator only if it is sincere. Recognizing workers' contributions goes a long way to increasing pride on the job. This applies to co-workers, juniors, and superiors. Everyone needs praise and encouragement. Just be sure you avoid buttering up superiors, and condescending to colleagues and those you manage. Being insincere produces disastrous results here.

Everything that contributes to productivity is important. Creating special awards on a regular basis that recognize these contributions is effective. Some people have been able to live with pride for years on making Salesman of the Month. It's important to recognize good citizenship, leadership, initiative, excellent safety records, and attendance. But don't get too caught up in the officialization of this recognition. In the Soviet Union, workers receive copious rewards for increases in productivity that have little effect on overall production. Too many awards lose their effectiveness. When everyone is a hero, no one is a hero. People need individual gratification for such incentives to work.

Ultimately, it is each worker's personal sense of responsibility that keeps productivity high. The best reward is in knowing, without having to ask anyone else, that your work is good, and valued. In the final analysis, it is probably impossible to make someone responsible or even productive for long by external rewards or punishments.

The most productive companies give people the chance to find themselves. This is the best business.

Few actions have as much positive effect as expressing praise and gratitude appropriately, and there is hardly any more damaging action than withholding well-deserved appreciation. Some employers and managers are reluctant to give workers praise because they fear they will be expected to pay more salary or a bonus for every piece of good work or new idea. This faulty thinking misses the point, but is unfortunately pervasive throughout the work world. Too many people in positions of power have risen to their post through greed and competitiveness and do not understand what really motivates people.

If you are reluctant to give encouragement, you are more likely to have workers who feel cheated and so demand monetary compensation. Be appreciative and natural in responding to others' efforts and give them feedback that reinforces them. The object of praise is to validate good work and strengthen the worker's positive sense of him or herself.

There are scores of books, studies, services, motivational experts, and employee recognition plans that offer help in raising productivity, but they run the risk of becoming thinly veiled manipulations. If workers feel used, they also feel obliged to get even. The subtlest way of getting even is to slow down. Negative attitude spreads through a work force like a bad rumor. It is more pervasive, for resentment is often as silent as it is deep. Feeling cheated, ignored, and unrecognized destroys morale and is difficult to repair. Expressing the praise that is due people is only a first step. People also need the opportunity to develop into and give their best. Being honest is the catalyst of any productive work force. Being fair is the magic ingredient.

The most productive work environment is ultimately the most humane and respectful one. There are ways to help employees identify with company goals and work as a team, but nothing is as powerful as respecting the individual person and encouraging and valuing his personal contribution. When people feel best about themselves, they produce the most and do their best work.

Chapter Eleven _____

TAKING CRITICISM

Nobody's perfect. Sooner or later you're going to make a mistake. Some of the time it will be noticed and commented upon. The way you react to criticism limits you more than perhaps any other reaction in business.

The most difficult job for many managers is to criticize an employee's behavior or job performance. Often they dislike making such criticisms more than the employee dislikes receiving them. Frequently, they don't have all the facts and have only second-hand reports, but know something isn't the way they expect it to be. So they are forced to come to you with an incomplete understanding and therefore their position is always a little shaky. They need information, to define errors and correct mistakes. It is like walking into the enemy's camp and asking for assistance in locating the most vulnerable place in their defenses.

Almost all people offer some resistance to admitting they were wrong. When people make excuses to rationalize their behavior and performance, they may think they are making a strong case, but supervisors see them as unwilling to learn or change, and as giving them a hard time. Resisting criticism causes stress and wastes energy and time. People who take criticism poorly, even though they may otherwise be doing a good job, are often the most difficult people for management to deal with. These are the people who keep them up late at night, the ones they want to let go, the bones in their throat. You are more trouble than you are worth if you offer resistance to valid criticism. If you don't take criticism well, your days are numbered, no matter what you may think.

The secret of taking criticism is to turn the situation into one where you are asking for advice. Your value is largely determined by the way you deal with your mistakes. That is your capacity for growth. The person who continually makes the same small mistakes, no matter what is said to him, is the loser; while the person who profits from a big mistake, learns his lesson, and moves on is the success.

If you try to avoid making mistakes at all costs, you are making a bigger mistake than the one you are trying to avoid. When you are overly cautious, you lose your spontaneity to experiment and your ability to adapt. Playing it safe is always a big mistake.

The people who are going to amount to anything make mistakes and they make them all the time. They just admit their errors and learn from them.

Of course, the source of the criticism is important. If you don't trust the other person, it is unlikely that you will be open to anything he says. You'll tend to see his intent as injurious rather than helpful and be likely to reject even his well-founded comments.

Negative people are the worst critics. They stalk their prey, waiting for a chance to express their vengeance. Dealing with negative people who have a legitimate complaint is especially difficult because they tend to abuse their leverage and express whatever negativity happens to be in their emotional pipeline. They feel that because they've caught you red-handed they now have an excuse to dump everything onto you. It's easy to get dragged into conflicts at moments like this, when you're put on the defensive. Just when you shouldn't, you are most likely to put up a fight. That's what most unreasonable arguments are about in the first place, combatting negativity while struggling to hide your flaws. Negative people try to provoke others to fight when they have a defensible case against them. Don't get trapped.

When negative people criticize you, think of yourself as a matador sidestepping an attacking bull. Offer no resistance. Keep your distance. Be nimble. It is necessary to observe and stay detached. Remember that whatever you have done has tapped into their reservoir of unexpressed anger and so they are likely to blow it up out of proportion. Don't take it personally or retaliate by criticizing their outburst. It will only enrage them further. Like all people who hold in anger, negative people have a low self-esteem. They bear grudges, express anger by proxy, displacing it on anyone they happen to catch in a mistake. If you resist, you will be the target of their negative outburst and trapped in the wrong issues. Remember, they have a case.

All of this is a momentous waste of time and a study in frustration that will leave you completely drained and feeling angry. Worse, you will have sunk to their level and your self-esteem will fall.

Minimize such conflict by being open. Let their comments pass through you. Interview them. Question them. Let them feel free to criticize and express their feelings. Help them be clear. Ask their advice. Although they'll be using you as their emotional whipping boy, think of yourself as healthier than they are and realize that by not reacting to their unreasonable attack you are acting in your own best interests.

Always remember in dealing with unreasonable or negative people that their hostility is really their problem even if you are their target. Even if they have power and authority over you, it is still your responsibility to keep them from polluting your consciousness. Don't fight with them. You can never win.

It's important to remember that most of the people who will criticize you are reasonable and still won't feel comfortable doing so. So put yourself in their position. Think how you can make their job easier.

Consider the way you react to criticism.

How receptive are you? Do you interrupt or interject comments like "I know," "Okay," or "I'll do it" before you have given the other person a chance to state his or her case? If you already know what the other person is trying to tell you, why didn't you correct yourself beforehand? So don't automatically challenge the other person and make his job more difficult. Don't become elusive.

Avoid being defensive.

A successful person listens to all comments without getting in their way or trying to influence or criticize the critic. If the critic is wrong, his point of view can still teach a lesson. The critic is just giving his report. Rather than fight with it, try to understand how it was framed and the forces that influenced it. Learn from it.

Be easy to deal with. Admit you were wrong. This lowers stress immediately and opens the way for constructive suggestions. If the critic is forced to spend his time trying to convince you that something is wrong, he'll have less help to offer. When you resist he doesn't know if you are being difficult, stupid, incompetent, insecure, uncooperative, sullen, or are just a loser. If you see yourself as someone on the way up, you don't want any of these negative attributes associated with your name.

Be sure you understand the complaint.

Take time to know the other person's concerns. Give your full attention and ask questions to be sure you understand.

Agree with the truth. Although this sounds simple, it establishes a sense of mutuality and paves the way for agreement.

Admit what you don't know. If you knew more you probably wouldn't have made the mistake you did, so you need more information. How well did you understand what was happening? What got in your way? When should you have asked for help? Why didn't you?

Ask for clarification.

The purpose of criticism is to make repairs. Be sure you understand what the other person thinks is wrong. Ask why he believes what he does, not to refute him but to become party to his thinking. If he knows something that you don't, he was able to see a mistake that escaped your awareness. You want to know how he knew what you didn't and what blocked your vision. This is important. If you don't understand this, you are likely to repeat the same mistakes. If you continually need supervision, you won't be seen as a potential leader. The leader differs from the follower in that he is aware of his limitations and overcomes them.

Ask for instructions and advice.

Be teachable.

Validate the efforts of the people who are trying to show you a better way.

Challenge is the incentive to growth. The athlete who does not push himself to pain does not exceed himself. If you accept challenges and continually reach to do your best, your work will become your own personal struggle and you will evolve as a person. It won't matter if your boss is narrow-minded or if your job doesn't really suit you. Your acceptance of challenge will lead you to where you are supposed to go. You will grow in spite of everything. Any challenge well taken will provide the right lessons. You are always the victor when you give everything.

After you are criticized, be still for a few minutes and consider all the ways you can put the advice into action. Don't hide from the obvious. You can pretend that the conversation never took place or try to rationalize your behavior and make the other person wrong, but if you do you become the loser when you make the same mistakes again.

Give feedback.

If you're still having difficulties, be the first one to bring them up. Keep the process of correction and growth open. Use the newly opened lines of communication to broaden the working relationship. Share your progress with supervisors. This increases their involvement and your value to them. Also, when you respond positively to their leadership, they feel more effective and their self-esteem also increases.

Accept and use criticism as an opportunity to rise to your best and to show others that you are ready to move on. A positive attitude is essential.

Turn criticism into an opportunity. Ask for advice. Be open, accepting, and expect to grow.

Chapter Twelve

GIVING CONSTRUCTIVE CRITICISM

I t is often more difficult to give criticism than receive it. People are naturally inhibited about telling other people what is wrong with their work. They don't want to hurt others' feelings and are afraid of being rejected when they point out a truth others may be unwilling to face. When giving criticism in business is seen as offering instruction or explanation, it usually presents little difficulty; but sometimes it can be even more problematic than in a personal relationship. Because business criticism is prompted by necessity, it is often neglected until severe problems develop and is then given abruptly and under stressful circumstances, so that it is equated with failure.

To prevent this supervisors should try to keep an objective distance, so that they can be effective and yet stay in contact. However, business settings are not spontaneous and there is a tendency to withhold criticism along with other feelings. Instead of pointing out errors as soon as they are noticed, even experienced supervisors tend to wait until they have enough data to warrant risking a confrontation. As a result they may wait too long, allowing workers to get into more serious trouble before they comment. As difficulties grow, workers feel more self-conscious about their mistakes and are likely to be increasingly defensive about hearing corrections.

The scene is set for conflict.

When a supervisor withholds criticism, he or she experiences discomfort and irritation. These feelings build, raising the risk of overreaction when the opportunity to criticize finally presents itself. At such times problems can be blown out of proportion and sometimes the wrong person becomes the target of the withheld criticism. Giving criticism improperly has remarkable power to create an atmosphere of alienation, resentment, and inefficiency.

If you have kept communication open by taking every opportunity to praise the good work you see, you shouldn't have any problem in pointing out shortcomings when they arise. Criticism and praise have to go hand in hand. If you only talk about mistakes, the people you supervise will expect to suffer a blow to their self-esteem whenever they see you approach. They will hide or be defended and you'll have difficulty being heard, no matter how good your advice.

The first rule is to make your criticism an extension of some praise. Although it's a good idea to reinforce good work as it happens, negative behavior is more likely to get your attention. The basic reason for criticism is to see that the squeaky wheel gets the oil. We focus on weaknesses, not because we are negative, but because pain is our greatest teacher. We are designed by nature to pay attention to danger and to take action to protect ourselves. When things go well, everyone is pleased to take credit for doing his or her share, but when there is a problem, people look to hide their deficiencies and deny their role in the downturn. Although people know they have room for improvement, they publicly deny their weaknesses, while secretly dwelling on their shortcomings as they question their competence and fear discovery. In the absence of openness people blame others and search for a scapegoat. It is important in approaching the squeaky wheels in business that you are aware of this. Oil the squeaky wheel, but examine and adjust the others as well.

Your goal in offering correction is to create a more open work atmosphere in which criticism and praise flow along as part of the work, where people do not dread being singled out, but expect and are pleased to receive attention and instruction when they need it. The following guidelines should help you to give constructive criticism.

Have clear objectives.

Before you criticize someone, know what you want to accomplish. At the top of your list should be to establish better, more open communication. You probably won't be able to make all the suggestions or corrections you want, but if you can open the channel between you and the other person, you have opened up the process of working out the problem together. If you don't establish this open relationship, it will continue to remain your biggest obstacle.

If you begin to criticize without knowing what you want to achieve, you are asking for trouble. You risk precipitating a blowup. Keep in mind that having a lot of criticisms to make reflects a closed relationship, one in which negative feelings have been building inside both parties. So be diplomatic and deliberate. You are really opening up your relationship to a greater depth of honesty. This has long been neglected, so be slow and gentle. Pick the time and place.

You want to be heard. You need to get through. So don't set up a situation that is designed to work against you. Avoid meeting with someone just before quitting time when he is already anxious to leave. This will add to his discomfort. Avoid meeting before meal breaks. People get grumpy when they are hungry and their stress tolerance drops.

Pick a place that is private, convenient, and friendly. You want the other person to hear you and put your comments into action. Put yourself in the other person's place. Consider the effect of making your comments in the setting you have chosen. Harsh public criticism alienates everyone and creates a closed, mistrusting atmosphere. When a fellow employee is treated unfairly, it threatens other workers. Embarrassing or humiliating others always works against you. First of all it is a cruel, punitive act and an abuse of power. It will be seen as heavy-handed and unfair even if the criticism is justified.

Be positive.

Because everyone has some dread of being discovered, it's best to begin by establishing and reinforcing the positive ties between you. People are less able to pay attention when they are afraid. Expressing your appreciation for their efforts reduces anxiety and thus lowers defenses.

View the problem as an entity in its own right. Talk about the problem with distance and encourage the other person to comment on it from the same perspective. The object is to acknowledge that a problem exists and establish a way of talking about it that produces results rather than increases conflict.

If the other person doesn't admit that there is a problem, present your evidence simply and without emotion. If you've been withholding criticism for a while, this is the moment when you run the greatest risk of losing control. The older your complaints, the less immediate and believable your criticism will sound. The other person will have poorer memory for distant events and will be less willing to concede your points and may even resent you for bringing up old issues.

This is a good time to restate your original goals to see if you both share the same understanding. Explain that you want to review the problem from the beginning and that you didn't comment earlier because you believed the problem would clear up. Admit that your judgment was wrong because the problem has persisted. Accept some of the blame for the problem. This creates a feeling of mutual concern. Perhaps you were misunderstood. Perhaps you did not express yourself clearly or failed to make sure that the other person really understood you. Maybe the other person did not feel comfortable approaching you when he first noticed the problem. Perhaps you seemed critical. In any case, make this an opportunity for both of you to develop closer cooperation in the future by stressing openness.

Once you both agree that something is wrong, allow the other person to share his perception of the problem. Interrupt as little as possible. Use short questions to direct him, such as "How did that happen?" "What was your reasoning?" or "What did you think was happening?" Inviting the other person to critique his own behavior is also effective. Asking how the work could be improved or similar mistakes prevented permits him to make suggestions in a friendly atmosphere. This allows you to see how he examines his performance. The strong worker is aware of his shortcomings and is working on them even before you point them out. He is pleased to discuss the problem and welcomes your instruction. The weak worker avoids examining the problem and denies his relationship to it.

Your job in offering correction is to help people look at themselves and take responsibility for their own improvement. Provide support and praise them when they improve. Encourage others to ask for your guidance. Get involved when others ask. Listen, pay attention, and show the same sincerity and cooperation you expect from them.

Make your point simply and directly. Make sure that you both are talking about the same subject. Restate your opinion and be done with it. If you find yourself in the same situation over and over again with the same person, then you have to consider if the other person is correctable. You should state this concern directly and see if doing so frees the other person to cooperate with you. If the situation cannot be corrected, you need to decide if it is in your best interest to have that person working for you.

The people who have the most trouble correcting others don't want to spend the time it requires, and tend to see employees as things to be managed, not as people. No one rules successfully by fiat. When you give demanding, impersonal orders other people may agree to your face but do whatever they can get away with when your back is turned.

Fear is a poor motivator. It inspires caution without introspection and makes people seek choices that limit their exposure rather than encouraging them to contribute their best. Growing requires risk and fear inhibits this. If you want others to work without constant supervision, give them the freedom to make mistakes without the threat of retaliation. Shouting and fright tactics won't make a sullen worker conform or free a reluctant person to give his or her best. People generally adapt to threats by becoming inefficient, not more productive.

When you're done, thank the other person for listening. Reassure him of your continued support and belief in his worth. If you have just put the other person on trial and are now giving him a last chance, it is especially important to do this. Expressing your positive belief at a time like this can make the difference between his sincerely trying or giving up. If you are not willing to give him a second chance to redeem himself, you might as well call it a day right then.

Make future contact easier by scheduling regular follow-up meetings so that you can monitor progress without creating a disturbance. Giving criticism without providing follow-up is poor management and reflects the manager's inability to see a project to completion. It may also indicate why the work ran into difficulty in the first place.

If your advice has not been accepted or doesn't seem to make any difference, you should deal with your failure to communicate matter-of-factly. Question whether your criticism was wrong or your advice ineffective. Be open about this and bring it up as a way to continue investigating the problem at hand. If the other person resists accepting responsibility, denies that a problem exists, or refuses to do what needs to be done, their days with you are limited. Don't threaten, don't cajole. This is a time for being resolute, for being surgical in your intention.

There is a limit to the number of chances anyone gets in life and everyone needs to learn their lessons. Be prepared to be clear in teaching yours by avoiding personal involvement or confusing emotions.

Chapter Thirteen _____

PLAYING WITH FIRE: SEX IN THE OFFICE

_____

The last thing in the world you want to do is to become sexually involved with someone with whom you work. Hear that. Believe it. Accept it. It is the single most disastrous move you can make in business no matter who you are or what you do.

It's poison.

Sex alters the power structure. It gives people power over you who have no business having power over you. Sexual involvement always comes from need and when that need is fulfilled you lose power. Once lost, it can never be recovered.

You do not even need to act on your sexual feelings for this loss of power to occur. All you have to do is state your sexual need for another person and you've lost it.

If you permit yourself to fall in love with someone who works for you, you give that person control over you. People who have any intelligence at all will refuse your advances. People who are cruel will lead you around by the nose. In time you'll lose respect for yourself for putting yourself in such a precarious position.

Once you have sexual relations with someone in your office, you are on a totally different basis. Men who use their employees like a personal harem are on borrowed time. A reputation of sexual promiscuity always causes disrespect in business.

With sexual intimacy there is an inevitable loss of distance between you and the people you are trying to manage. Word travels fast. It only takes one little leak to tarnish your reputation and destroy your credibility. Long dictation sessions behind locked doors in the middle of the day are a demoralizing absurdity to everyone else and mark you as a child who cannot find sex on his or her own without using leverage.

As soon as you have sex with a co-worker, you risk losing the other person as a friend. No matter who is having sex with you on company time, they are expecting something in return. If you think it is your charm or cleverness that has won your conquest, you're only kidding yourself.

Having sex in the office is an abuse of power for both parties. Having sex in the office is also an abuse of self because you are really not being seen for yourself. The reaction you are getting is to your mask, your position.

Sometimes sexual relations begin because of boredom. Sexual feelings exist everywhere; when things seems dull, minds wander. Expressing some sexual feelings as playful teasing is just part of the normal male-female polarity that exists whenever the sexes meet. It is without real meaning, chemical in nature, and not to be taken seriously. Everyone in the work situation is putting on what sportscasters call their "game face." It's not the way they really are. It's merely the way they act. People at work try to please and be accepted. Sexual banter is a common form of recreation.

Sexual contact, however, whether it is a pinch or a grab, is way off limits. It is beyond the game of friendly kidding. While talking about who was with whom the night before is permissible as part of the normal recess talk, expressing an actual sexual desire for someone is a violation. It introduces the most vulnerable feelings of all into an atmosphere where feelings have the lowest priority.

Sexual contact in the office is always a sign of desperation. Hardly anyone who has had a sexual alliance at work has their life together. If you are sexually involved at work, you are nuts and I'm telling you straight out. You are going to pay for it and it is going to make your life miserable.

Anyone you have sex with in business has something over you. If that person is unhappy, you have a time bomb in your career. While someone may tolerate abuses of all other kinds without saying a word, people are remarkably spiteful in taking revenge for sexual abuse. It is always ugly. Sex and power may be attracted to each other, but they degrade the partners in a work setting and mark each participant as a rank amateur, if not an outright loser.

Having an affair with a customer is a degrading practice. Unfortunately, it's common and it always shortens the business relationship even though both parties may deny it.

One-night stands are the sign of an unhappy person who needs the anonymity and shelter of transiency to keep from committing himself. If you are on the make all the time you are away from home, it doesn't say much about your life, your stability, or your values.

If you think that you can improve your position by having sex at work, you are operating under a delusion that will eventually destroy you. First of all, no matter what you feel, probably neither of you is in love. Would you put someone you really loved into the jeopardy and under the stress that a love relationship in the office does? The people who become involved with you in a business setting will also become uninvolved just like that. If you try to press your luck and insist on the relationship continuing, or on otherwise benefiting from it, for example by profiting from your silence, you are soon going to be looking for another job.

If you become involved in sex in the office, you will deserve exactly what you get.

It's never worth it.

Occasionally, relationships that begin at work do turn out successfully, but such cases are in the minority.

Becoming involved in the office often means committing adultery. Should you get caught at it, you are discovered to be unfaithful, a homewrecker, and a risky investment for the company.

Sexual involvement in the office is a difficult secret to keep. You are likely to be reported by jealous co-workers and envious competitors.

If you love someone at work, you do them no favor. Your support of their opinions will only be seen as favoritism and will not be taken seriously. Your disagreements will be seen as lovers' quarrels.

Should the relationship dissolve, you have little room for recovery. You are trapped in a rigid environment in which the added stress caused by the hurt and secrecy will decrease your efficiency. In such circumstances it is common for one of the partners to quit or be fired.

Love affairs distance fellow employees, making them feel resentful for being kept on the outside of an intimate relationship.

Others will see you as irresponsible, especially if you break up the team: for example, if you are management who happens to fall in love with a union member.

How can you avoid sexual relationships in the office?

Say no.

Treat sexual advances like a joke.

The best way to end a relationship in the office is to admit it was a terrible mistake. Express regrets without assigning

147

blame. If the other person can't relinquish his or her affections, your job may be in danger. If this sounds a little too severe, then you are beginning to understand the game you are playing. After all, business is business.

While it is sometimes possible to reestablish a friendship after an office affair is over, jealousy, insecurity, loathing, and resentment are often the most common residuals and usually prevent it. It's important to have a good talk after the affair is over, but if the affair was between unequals, the chances of getting a thorough airing of the issues and coming to friendly terms again are slight.

Once the sexual barrier has been crossed, there is usually no return to normal. At best it takes two well-adjusted, determined people who care about each other and respect their mutual positions to maintain a friendship under such circumstances. But such people wouldn't start a sexual relationship at work in the first place. The chances are you'll be lucky to get out of the situation on speaking terms. Transfer or a new job is far more likely.

If you continue on after the affair, the opportunities for exploitation and abuse are ever present. Even if they are not acted upon they present continual obstacles to clear communication and cooperation. A past affair has a way of preoccupying people and making them less able to concentrate.

Unfortunately, the usual solution to such problems is to move on. But then, how do you explain a premature change of job to a future employer? You'll give the impression of something going wrong, act closed, and so give a potential employer reason to suspect you.

If you discover that some of your employees are sexually involved, consider your discovery in the light of what this implies about their usefulness to your organization, and if you see it interfering with their jobs, bring it up to them individually. No matter how fair you try to be, the chances are that you will end up letting go the least important of the two.

There is no way that having sex in the office can be in your best interest. So if you are having sex at work, I know a good psychiatrist you should see.

Chapter Fourteen _____

THE PSYCHOLOGY OF NEGOTIATION

_____

The ABC's of Persuading Others

Learning to negotiate successfully requires an understanding of many of the issues already discussed in this book. You need to know yourself and your goals. You need to be able to interview others to discover their basic needs and understand what motivates them. You cannot understand the message without understanding the messenger. You need to be able to run a meeting efficiently, to think creatively and flexibly under pressure. You need to be realistic about the limitations of others yet determined to get results. You need to be selfish and to feel deserving of winning, and yet be compassionate of the feelings of others and responsive to them.

What follows is not a textbook for negotiating but a collection of rules and principles for putting into action what you already have learned here.

Your attitude is important. You need to believe that you deserve to win. No matter how strong your position, having self-doubts going into a negotiation will cost you points. You need to project a feeling of worth, a belief that your demands are reasonable and that you are a reasonable person who is willing to listen to others. You want to avoid overstating your case, acting entitled, or expecting others to roll over and submit just because you want something.

You also need to believe that the other party deserves to win, too. You need to abandon the concept that you and the other side are adversaries and that one must lose and one must win. This kind of thinking creates unresolvable impasses. You must create a situation where both parties gain.

Establish your objectives. If you don't know what you want when you go into a negotiation, you won't know when you have won. The following exercise will help you decide what is really important to you. Make a shopping list four columns wide. In the first column, write down the points you want to win. In the next column, put down the reason why you want each item and why you think you deserve it. In the third column, indicate the other party's probable objection to your point. And in the last column, write a response to that objection, showing how that party's resistance can be met. This takes a bit of thought so don't rush. You need this preparation. Although you might, it is unlikely that you will come up with a great idea under pressure during the negotiation. So think your arguments through and support them solidly. If you are asking for more money and you suspect you will be told that the other party can't afford it, be prepared to show how your productivity and profitability warrant the increase. No one is going to reward you just because you feel you should be rewarded. Hard facts, documented evidence, reasons that justify actions, are needed. Value yourself and give positive weight to every contribution you make that proves your point.

Know what is important to you. Rank the items on your list from vital to unimportant. What must you have and why? What can you give away? What must you hold onto to avoid being damaged? Past what concession will further discussion be counter-productive? When should you walk out?

If you don't know when you would walk out, you have no business going into a negotiation.

Do the same for the other party. Anticipate his moves. Make his list of demands, arrange it in his order of priorities, survey his arguments, and prepare counterarguments. How will he expect you to argue your points? When will he walk out? Try to determine what the other party will consider a victory. What points must he win? What issue does he value most? Try to understand his strategy. He has a plan, too. What is it?

Make some estimate of what you think the other person will be willing to give. Look at his list again. What does he want and why does he want it? What can he easily give away that you want?

Make sure you are aware of what the other party values even if he never mentions it. Being aware of and addressing his basic needs develops mutuality, while ignoring these needs creates a gulf. While these basic needs have been discussed before, they have special importance in negotiations.

People are concerned with having a home, a sense of participation, a feeling of belonging, emotional consistency, and peace.

They want control, power, freedom, and financial security.

They need praise and recognition.

Some of these items can be given away without great cost to you. For example, giving a creative person freedom is often worth more than money. Think about others' needs before making an offer. A point that you may not even value may mean a great deal to the other party.

Understand what the other person thinks is reasonable and unreasonable. These limits are helpful to guide you.

Determine the total pie to be divided. This is not always easy to do because concealing facts is common in negotiations. Even so, try to find out as much as you can. If you go into a negotiation asking for a fixed amount without understanding how it relates to the entire picture, you are placing yourself at a disadvantage. If your demand is excessive, you will get a costly education. Then, as you sheepishly lower your demands, you may end up getting much less than you would have had you been reasonable. On the other hand, if you underestimate the total amount available and ask for too little, you will be seen as naïve and will probably be beaten down even further.

Be prepared to bargain for everything. Don't decide to give anything away automatically, even those items at the bottom of your list. Use these as bargaining chips to sweeten the deal and make it go your way. Establish the value of these items in relationship to others' needs. Unless you are making a calculated gesture of goodwill, don't give items away up front, but allow others to ask for them. Giving in response to others' needs places you in a position of power, and then you can ask for something in return without diminishing your position. Whereas when you offer too freely, you appear to lower the value of the thing you give.

If you think that this advice is a bit too calculated and contrived and that the best plan should be to reveal your hand openly, you have the wrong idea about negotiating. When other people come to play the game, they expect you to play as well. Remember, many of the people you will deal with do not come from a win-win position and will need to be humored as you educate them.

In a negotiation the value of the thing that is won is often determined by the difficulty involved in winning it. So when you see the other party resisting a point you wish to win, avoid pressing directly. It will only increase the value of the point and make it harder to win. Determine what the other party's resistance means. It could reflect a cash flow or credit problem. People hold onto unreasonable negotiating positions when they are desperate or are afraid of losing. When others get stuck in a position, identify their needs and see if you can come up with

153

a new solution to their problem. Be flexible and prepared to adapt to their situation rather than insist on them meeting your demands. Perhaps they can't. Maybe they're too afraid. They only see their problem. You seek a solution. Point out mutual interests and work toward them. Having some negotiating chips in reserve will come in handy here.

Remember, anything you have that the other party needs, lacks, or wants is a negotiating point. This includes the use of your name, talent, goodwill, patronage, customers, past performance, salesmanship, special skills, leadership, hardware, space, time, labor, territory, credit line, manufacturing capability, contacts, knowhow, recipe, formula, patent, copyright, license, right of way, lease, mortgage, leverage, position, experience, friends, influence, experience, power, good looks, or public relations support. Anything that you have that is of value in solving the other person's problem is valuable to you in a negotiation. Value it and use it.

Decide what to keep secret. A negotiation is not a time for openness. Some things need to be concealed. If certain knowledge would give the other party power, it should remain secret. Don't give out information unnecessarily, especially if viewing it out of context might create a negative impression. Stress your strongest points, but if there are negative points that are bound to come out, bring them up first when you have the floor and make your best case. Waiting until they are brought up by the opposition always puts you at a disadvantage and is a weakness.

Anticipate losses. It's important to have some idea of the points you won't be able to win so that you are not caught by surprise during discussions and demoralized. Be prepared to concede these inevitable losing points and gain power by treating your concession as if it were a gift to the other side. Giving away generously what cannot be won will work in your favor as a demonstration of your reasonableness.

Choose a hospitable location for the negotiation. Don't be afraid to choose a setting that puts the other party at ease. Attempts at power manipulations of space, chairs, and so on are really empty-headed exercises by people who do not have much confidence in themselves. If you feel comfortable and unthreatened, you can easily have a meeting on the other person's turf without giving anything away.

The best rule is to make the setting unobtrusive and its choice uneventful. Allow for the most convenient participation of key people who have the power to say yes. Too often negotiations are conducted with people who do not have the power to make decisions, but only to submit recommendations, necessitating another negotiation later on. Placing a buffer between you and the person you should be talking to is especially common in the automobile business where the salesman has to check with the sales manager to see if he can accept your offer. This breaks negotiating momentum by creating inertia. Be sure you set up the negotiation with the right people.

Avoid game playing as much as possible. Too many businessmen are so driven to win that they end up getting less than they would have if they had been flexible. When someone has to win, a skillful negotiator will figure out all the ways to allow this to happen and trade them to his advantage, putting up a fight in each case, just to give the impression of losing.

The Negotiating Procedure

RULES

It is sometimes useful to make rules concerning the negotiation, for example, outlining procedures or protocol, but this is more applicable for large contract negotiations than for simple attempts of two parties trying to strike a deal. However, in negotiations in which many volatile political or prejudicial elements threaten to disrupt the proceedings, rules are useful to keep the flow of ideas open and to permit disagreements to be fully aired with the lowest risk of discussions breaking off.

ROLES

If you are part of a negotiating group, even a small group consisting of two persons, you are a team and it is necessary that each person understands his or her role. You should not disagree with a team member unless the disagreement is strategically planned to win over the other side, such as where one member plays tough, the other conciliatory. This is the old good cop–bad cop tactic used to trick criminals into confessing. It is a manipulation and creates and presses an unfair advantage. It relies on intimidation and is typical of brainwashing techniques.

Roles should be decided beforehand. One member of the team should make the presentation, one should arbitrate; one should play devil's advocate, another the heavy. Playing roles establishes an identity, a sense of one person as spokesman. When the negotiation gets rough or the situation seems to deteriorate, it's possible to switch negotiators or negotiating roles and have the "reasonable" person take over from the "tough" negotiator and make a conciliatory offer. Establishing roles gives structure to a discussion and can create a negotiating opportunity out of a stalemate. Just be sure the roles don't get in the way of common sense or blind you from seizing the opportunity you are waitng for.

OPENING GAMBITS

It's helpful to begin by stating your view of the mutual needs and interests of both parties. This statement of commonality should be referred to throughout the negotiating process as a reminder of the higher goal you share. Keep this statement brief so that you can quote it easily and use its unifying power. It should be a highly positive statement: for example, to create a profitable working relationship, to make a deal that is in everyone's best interest, to disarm, to establish territorial limits, or to promote safety and understanding. It is helpful as you repeat this opening statement to acknowledge the other party's legitimate needs. Hearing someone express an understanding of your problem lowers defenses. Knowing that your concerns have been heard reduces the need to be belligerent just to be noticed.

In fact, most of the anxiety surrounding the negotiating procedure has to do with the fear of being ignored or misunderstood. Granting this understanding to the other party without making them fight for it gives them something they need, builds respect for your fairness, and leads others to be generously disposed to you. Often people end up at the negotiating table because this very same understanding was previously denied, leaving them feeling empty and cheated. As a result, they are often negotiating just to receive financial reparations for this injurious oversight. Granting them recognition, praise, or support, repairs the damage directly. If you doubt this, you don't understand human nature.

Present your case matter-of-factly, stating your point of view calmly and with a sense of the rightness of your position, explaining each point as you make it. Give the other person the same opportunity.

Although this has been mentioned before, it is never as important as at this juncture to be an attentive listener. Many of the positive benefits of negotiating come through the release of pent-up feelings. If you cut off this expressive flow, you endanger the process. So be generous as you listen. Let the other person say what they need to say. Listening without planning to retaliate and being pleasant and understanding is being strong. It puts you in a superior position, not one from which you look down on the other party, but one of emotional strength. Letting a troubled person talk is exercising great and good power.

157

If you can accept this you have gained a critical edge. You do not have to respond. Just indicate that you have heard and understood.

Sometimes simply by listening to others make their point, you allow them to feel they have won. On the other hand, if you don't listen, the other party will feel the need to punish.

If you discover that the other people do not have a plan or seem disorganized, superimpose your plans over their confusion. You do this by offering to clarify their points and needs. Help them determine what they want and what matters to them. In fact, the most important part of negotiating with less skilled people is to help them define their goals and then to fulfill them at the lowest cost to yourself. Be sincere. Assume a helpful attitude and act like a partner, rather than an adversary; this will pay off best. If you challenge less competent people at their vulnerable points, they may feel trapped and become rigid. They may feel obliged to demonstrate their power by walking out or becoming unreasonable. When you challenge weak people, you risk bringing out the bully in them. They may abuse their power to precipitate a crisis just to assume control over you.

In dealing with such difficult people, be helpful. Be a teacher, Draw them out. Gently point out the problems they don't see and ask them how they want to handle them. This disarms them and allows you to frame the discussion to your advantage. While there is no denying that these tactics are manipulative, it is better to take control of a negotiation than to allow your interests to be trampled by others' incompetence and reflexive assertiveness.

Avoid confrontation over personality, morality, ethics, intention, or motivation.

If you cannot reach an agreement, do not be disheartened. Agree to disagree and view the present impasse as momentary. Restate your interest in working matters out and your belief that a solution beneficial to all parties is still possible. In the meantime, create an instrument of intent that expresses this common aim, even if it is informal such as a handshake.

Keep the door open.

When the other party feels entitled to more than you be-lieve he deserves, help him examine his position by asking and answering questions that explore the impact of his demands. Remind him that the bargain has to make sense for everyone involved and also indicate that if he didn't need other people he wouldn't be trying to make a deal with you.

Every person's perception of the world is unique and the present situation has developed along different lines for differ-ent parties. Getting others to share their perception is a heal-ing act and can reduce unreasonable demands considerably.

When a person feels entitled, he is unwilling to see others' positions. Spend the necessary time to clear the air. You will be wasting your time until you do because unreasonable peo-ple do not listen, they only defend.

It is also possible to mention the other people's weak points without appearing like the aggressor. You do this by pointing out the shortcomings of their position and immediately down-playing and forgiving them. Tell them you are aware of their weaknesses, and accept them, and are still prepared to do business with them. Sparing them the necessity of making their own points, you grant them an easy victory, but on your terms. Offer to correct their deficiencies with what you bring to the negotiation. Again, you must be sincere or you will sound pa-tronizing.

In a well-run negotiation everyone should come away feel-ing as if he has won. When you think about it, this is the only kind of settlement that stands a chance of success. If people walk out of a negotiation feeling cheated, manipulated, or con-trolled, whatever agreement has been reached is tainted with resentment and subject to further questioning and dispute. A successful negotiation brings people to a better understanding of themselves and others. They also feel better understood and relieved that their demands and aspirations are regarded as reasonable and that their needs are recognized as important. This matters every bit as much as gaining concrete concessions. To achieve financial demands without being treated like an equal or without being regarded as having worth does not feel very much like a victory. Respect and recognition can be given away cheaply. They can be denied only at great cost. A successful negotiation enhances feelings of common purpose and individual worth.

Sometimes it is not possible to win in a negotiation. There are times when the battle is lost and there is nothing to be gained by continuing the discussion. Each party must determine beforehand where this point is and gird himself to the possibility of acting on it by walking out. You should never walk out of a negotiation abruptly unless you are using the tactic to frighten an intransigent negotiating team into coming to its senses. This is not a delicate move and has great potential for making matters worse. Bear in mind that the people most likely to walk out as a tactic do so out of desperation because it is the only move they think they have left. It almost always signals your impulsiveness and unreasonableness to the other people. While it is sometimes true that the other side becomes locked in their own defensive posture and needs to come to the awareness that they really need you, and throwing a temper tantrum is the only way of getting them to see this, it is a procedure to be discouraged. If you must walk out, never do so in anger, but with great regret, acknowledging that continuation does not seem profitable.

Give points away when you feel they bring you closer to getting what you want. Realize that there are real points, which are matters of substance, and ego points, which are matters of pride. You should be willing to yield on emotional issues without much comment. Again, if you make your emotional needs negotiating points, you risk being bought off cheaply. Make these personal needs incidental, except that they will be met out of common courtesy and decency, and respond appreciatively when they are, but refer continually to more substantive issues while granting others all the strokes their fragile egos need. Then you are negotiating from strength and have the best change of getting what you want.

When you have what you want, you have won. Don't be overbearing or vindictive. Be grateful, express appreciation that the other party has listened and understood. Keep the door open for continuing discussions, and if there is still any unfinished business, define it in the new spirit of cooperation that has developed. Achieving one positive resolution often makes it possible to remove other roadblocks on less important issues. So use this good spirit to address other unresolved issues. You don't need to settle them right now, but merely state your belief that they too are now soluble. Like a drop of mercury coalescing with others to form a greater totality, let the good of a positive negotiation seek out other good and build on a momentum of understanding.

Chapter Fifteen _____

ENHANCING CREATIVITY

Understanding the creative person and the creative process will increase your productivity. Learning to encourage creative people and manage them effectively is always in your best interest. Whenever you make an environment hospitable to creative people you become more creative yourself. Whether this increased creativity is used to develop a new profit center, to discover a better way to market a product, or to invent a solution to a perplexing problem, it will result in unexpected benefit to you.

The greatest resource of a growing company is the creativity of the people who work for it. Creativity in everyday matters and problem solving determines, just as much as the development of major innovations, how profitable a company is. Most well-established companies survive on the strength of a single idea. As that idea ages, it tends to lose its effectiveness and relevance and the company ages with it. Company business structures mature and become more rigid. Just when older companies need new ideas most, they are the least able to inspire them and least hospitable to receive them.

When companies are young, everything feels possible. All ideas are welcomed. Experience is limited. The marketplace hasn't settled yet. Roles have not been clearly defined, so everyone feels free to speculate and contribute. Almost anything goes. Communication is informal. Meetings are problem-related. People are involved and on their toes. In a start-up situation the creative surge of building something new fills everyone with anticipation. There's a general feeling of accomplishment and worth. The direction is forward. People feel encouraged to participate at their best. These are exciting times.

As companies age they become less free. Departments form and become established in their ways of doing business and handling situations. Curiosity and open-mindedness is replaced by convention. Rather than seeking new solutions, management assumes that what worked once must be right. A standard procedure is defined and deviations from it are viewed with alarm. Conformity replaces creativity. In time the same boldness that was once valued and necessary to create the original idea is viewed as rebellious, dangerous to the best interests of the company, and is discouraged. Although change is feared, expansion is cherished. Because growth is seen as expansion of the old ways and innovation for innovation's sake is discouraged, companies tend to reach their limits and become consumed by themselves. It becomes ever more expensive to expand against inertia. Improvements are preferred to discovery. They are safer and more predictable than real change. The reins are drawn tighter. Rules, proper channels, layers of authority, chains of command, replace spontaneity. Communication is more formal. Meetings center around policy and image. The main thrust of corporate thinking is to preserve the system. In such an environment, creativity dies a slow death. Buying a younger company is sometimes the best idea an older company can come up with.

And yet management in such companies would probably insist that they welcomed creativity. They may even believe that,

163

but the truth is that although most companies would like to find creative solutions to their problems, very few know how to encourage creativity or provide an atmosphere that nurtures ideas. In fact, much of what fosters creativity is outlawed by companies as a matter of policy. And most of them don't even know it!

To begin with, because creativity is a function of a single person, increasing a company's creativity requires dealing with the creative person as an individual. Companies are not creative. The individuals who work for them are. While creative people must be team players to be effective in business, they need to be individual to be creative.

Everyone has some creative ability. Like everything else, creativity varies in degree from person to person, and in the individual from day to day and from one time of life to another. All artists have an early, middle, and late period in which their style changes and often their manner of working as well. Creativity and play are very much linked. In fact, it could be said that the creative artist maintains his childlike nature, but adds discipline to it.

Creativity begins where logic ends. You work on a problem until you get stuck. Where do you go after you have run out of options, when no answer satisfies your needs, when the rules don't point to a solution? The answer is, you make something up. Inventing possibilities in a playful, unthreatening environment that encourages the game of "Let's pretend" is the tactic most likely to produce a workable creative result, while demanding answers shuts off creative thinking.

You cannot command a group of workers to solve a problem creatively any more than you can insist that a group of children have a good time playing. All you can do is see that the environment is supportive, open, and uncritical. Many leaders feel too threatened to permit others the necessary freedom to create. It makes them feel out of control. They want clearly defined goals and predictable results. Such rigid thinking may be part of the problem. It's too narrow. Defining goals is only one step in the creative process. Intuitive thinking is needed, not logic that deduces the right answer like Sherlock Holmes.

The creative process is a leap from the known to the unknown. It is a risk taken in the belief that the creator will land on solid ground, even if he may invent that solid ground while he is in midair. The end result may not be a fully formed, specific idea, but just a notion of what might be, a direction. Mozart, when explaining how he wrote music, indicated that he just put down notes that the music suggested to him.

A creative notion works like an object you throw into the still pond of your mind. You must allow the notion to impact deeply within you by stating the problem as clearly as possible and then concentrate on the ideas the ripples bring to the surface.

Allowing your mind to follow any and all suggestions occurring to it is the key to creativity. Creative thinking happens naturally all the time, you only need to be free to tap into it. It's essential to avoid being judgmental or doubting and to surrender completely to the process of flowing from one idea to the next without censorship. The creator must be vulnerable and self-accepting.

Criticism and correction should be postponed until the creative idea is fully expressed or else the creative flow will stop. The creative process invents, improvises, and seeks variation. It does not correct itself. Correction involves taking distance. While creation may begin by removing oneself from the familiar in order to see it anew, the creative act requires total immersion, becoming the thing that is being created. It is relatively simple to learn how to edit and be critical, but you first need something with which to work. Creative people tend to be their own severest critics, but not when they are creating. If you see an artist critical of his work at the time of creation, you are probably seeing an artist with a creative block.

The shaping that occurs as the original idea is developing

is also creative. It is an open view of all the possibilities that the creative notion suggests to the creator, even the most far-fetched, silliest, impractical solution. Opening up the process so that the mind is free to receive its own ideas without prejudice or censorship is the method. The creative person is concerned only with the question, Does it work? Is this where that idea wanted to go? The question, Is it good? should be left to someone else, someone the artist calls his audience.

Creative people are often regarded as childlike or unbusinesslike because of their apparent lack of organization. This is a reflection of their spontaneity. They do not feel a need to hold their perceptions in any particular order. They tend to see the world as an assemblage of elements that someone put together to suit himself and, therefore, see no reason why they should not rearrange it for their own pleasure. They are not bound by convention or rules. They naturally ask, Why not? and need to be in this childlike state in order to create. It requires great discipline and hard work to achieve the correct frame of mind and maintain the innocence of perceiving the world anew. Picasso said he spent his entire adult life learning to paint like a child again.

To create, one needs, like a child, to become immersed in the energy of one's feelings and the impact of sensations and to use them as creative elements. Directing this creative energy to solve problems is not easy and sometimes not even possible. Often creative thoughts have little relevance to specific goals or needs and are merely part of the creative process. Many great ideas occurred by capitalizing on creative mistakes and having the sensibility to recognize them.

Understanding the creative person is the prerequisite for dealing with him or her effectively and for creating an atmosphere that enhances creative thinking.

How do you apply this knowledge in business? First, understand that any attempt to impose rigid limits on creative people is bound to meet with failure. Presenting general long-term goals and defining the problem clearly is more helpful.

It's also necessary to express trust in the other person and to give the freedom to improvise, to play at inventing solutions. The best way to use creative people is to use them to develop direction not necessarily product. If the direction is clear, the product will suggest itself and its adaptations will follow naturally. This has to be a matter of faith. You cannot judge the effectiveness of your creative people over the short term. There are fallow moments and creative spurts. Remember, much of what takes place during the act of creating is highly personal and although it may appear to be of little direct financial benefit it is a necessary part of the process.

It is essential to understand that keeping the creative process flowing is as important as the final product. Indeed, from the creative person's point of view, the final product is only a part of the process. While the company may reward the creative person for the results he achieves, he is rewarded more by the act of creating itself, by experiencing himself as creating. Artists frequently experience feelings of loss when they complete a work and become reluctant to finish what they have created, equating letting go with shutting down their creativity. Creating is an outward expression of feelings that expands a person's consciousness as he extends himself into the world. When that process closes down, the artist feels empty and isolated. The creative process had filled a space within the creator in much the same way that Keats suggested when he said of the poet that he was a nightingale who sang to keep from being lonely. For this reason it is always useful to have creative people work on several projects at once and at varying stages, just to keep the process of creativity open.

Every creative person initiates the creative process in his or her own way and needs the room to do what he must to get it started and sustain it. This can sometimes get quite bizarre. One successful playwright begins by visualizing a skeleton, lying on a dark landscape, with roses growing through its rib cage. A door

167

opens and a streak of light appears behind it. She looks into the light and sees the answers to her creative questions within it. This imaging process focuses her energy, and allows her to become one with her creative point of view. Some days she needs to repeat this exercise several times before her creative flow begins. Perhaps it seems silly or unnecessary, but because such rituals work, they should be left alone. Creative people demand a lot of themselves and need sympathy. A little indulgence goes a long way to enhancing creative performance.

Every creative person has his own style. To be most creative, a person needs to be most himself. This can lead to problems in tightly controlled business settings. When there is high expectation to conform, creative people become inhibited. The creative person may even be seen as rebellious or as endangering accepted practices and his work may be rejected without being given a fair chance.

Since the creative person's strength is to see the old anew and continually seek out what works best, he may threaten conservative people. Allowing someone to act and think like an individual may be too alien for aging companies that have a vested interest in maintaining the status quo. The fear of risking characterizes companies on the way out. Creative people, especially, do not function well there.

It is almost always a bad idea to interfere with someone's creative process. You're likely to cut off their flow and you'll be resented for it. While some creative people flourish in front of an audience, others are so retiring they can lose an entire day's work if someone merely knocks on their door. It is critical to allow for such individual variation. All creative people need uninterrupted work time and space. Don't diminish the value of such people by trivializing the negative effect of interrupting them.

Creative people fatigue under stress and while volume may increase, the quality drops. Such junk production may meet the demanding schedule forced on them, but it eventually undermines their self-esteem. They know better than anyone else when their work is good, and when it falls short, they often become blocked. Knowing how much pressure to apply and when takes skill, understanding, and more than that, respect for the artistic integrity of the creative person. Creativity cannot be rushed.

It is deceptively easy to intimidate and undermine creative people because emotionally they are a little childlike. It is always counterproductive to take advantage of this vulnerability, their stock in trade, because if they become protective, they shut down. They need to be totally open in their feelings in order to be receptive to the ideas that these feelings suggest to them. They need to maintain their sensitivity as they question their deficiencies and try to perfect them. Caring for details that others may not even notice makes all the difference to them. It's no wonder that they often wear their hearts on their sleeves. While they are often highly intelligent, they are full of uncertainty when involved in the act of creation, for then they are in the realm of the unknown, the untried, and the risky and are often operating at the far limits of their talent. They push themselves to their weakness and beyond.

They need to be supported as they ask their questions:

Does this work?

How do I do this?

Can this be simpler?

What am I trying to say?

Has this been done before?

Does this really matter?

Should I be doing something more universal and lasting?

Do I have the right to be so selfish?

Do I have the talent to do this, or am I just fooling myself?

Do I have the right technique?

It is important to realize that creative people really don't know the answers to these questions and that their questioning serves mainly to encourage their creative thinking. The creative process is asking questions in ever-increasing detail to everything that is sensed. At times of soul-searching, creative people may appear like pushovers, seem ambivalent, insecure or confused, and they may appeal to others for advice. It's best to resist giving them too much direction because their process is easily sidetracked.

Unless you have a better solution, avoid being critical. Even if their work seems wrong, resist commenting. Let them struggle. Be actively silent. Anticipate a solution. The struggle is part of their process, perhaps the most important part. The struggle gives them courage to let go. They need to take a risk, to open more, to abandon conventional thinking and come up with something new. Keep their process open by letting them suffer with what doesn't work. It will make the solution clearer to them.

If you must comment do so by asking nonjudgmental questions that they might ask themselves.

How does this work?

Where is this leading?

What other possibilities are you considering?

Why did you choose this?

Where do you want this to go?

What effect are you seeking?

Do you like this?

Again, because of their transparent vulnerability, there is a great temptation to try to manipulate creative people. There are equally great dangers in doing so. The people who are most likely to manipulate them mistake their vulnerability for weakness, when it is actually a measure of the flexible strength necessary to reach within and face the unknown. Creative people may show a lack of concern for mundane affairs and leave business to others, but this also reflects an inner focus, rather than a lack of aptitude. When a work situation becomes intolerable, they can suddenly manage the details, take over if necessary, and leave without shedding a tear.

The most important product that a creative person brings to any enterprise is the creative process itself. Staying in the process is the creative person's goal far more than it is to produce.

Maintaining this process requires:

Staying open.

Being prepared to receive and record inner suggestions.

Testing out notions without fear of failure.

Taking the time to do whatever needs to be done.

Permission to allow the creative process to run where it will, when it will, to be able to cancel meetings, meals, dates, appointments and obligations to make the thing happen.

No wonder it is so difficult to remain creative in the business world.

Things that kill creativity include:

Criticism, especially that based on envy.

Arbitrary deadlines. These can kill creativity, but for some people they enhance the process. There are last-minute creators who need the pressure of a deadline to take a creative risk and leap to a solution.

Rigid work schedules; rules.

Too much praise. Excessive approval, like criticism, can misdirect and divert the creative flow.

Editing as you go rather than just flowing with ideas.

171

Too much supervision, a need for progress reports, or excessive permissions needed to undertake work.

Things that foster creativity are:

Appreciation: sincere, timely, and unobtrusive.

Encouragement without its getting too specific. "I know you can do it" is enough.

Freedom to release whatever is in the creative pipeline seeking expression. Think of it as a kind of clearing the throat, keeping the process open.

Allowing for individual differences in taste and style.

Letting people stay in a comfortable creative frame of mind. If you can't grant this all the time, provide blocks of time without demands. It will pay off.

Creative Meetings

In a well-run creative meeting everyone feels open and gives their best. Here are some general principles for running an effective creative meeting.

Give the project an identity of its own. Loyalty should be directed to the project rather than to any individual or group. A creative team should be encouraged to look to its process for identity. Working productively is the goal.

All contributions should be judged impersonally. They either work or do not work.

The authorship of ideas should always be less important in judging them than their effectiveness. Just because a creative person comes up with an idea, doesn't automatically mean it is right. Creative people frequently produce ideas of lesser value just to keep their creative flow going. These ideas are often overestimated by others merely because of their source.

Other people whose creative input is likely to be overweighted include the boss, his offspring, financial backers, sponsors, clients, or external critics. There are obvious reasons for this prejudice, including others' need to please and flatter, to be accepted, and to seek advancement. Playing on these needs denies the project its own identity and fragments the creative process into personal factions. Such rubber-stamping works against inventing new solutions, the reason for holding such a meeting in the first place.

In every creative meeting, one person should assume the role of director. This role need not be invested with authority. The leader should merely direct, making sure the meeting covers all of the points on the agenda and addresses the problems it was called to help solve. He or she should enhance the flow of ideas, encourage, support, and nurture rather than act as a decision maker. It is useful for the director to restate goals, question how contributions lead to solutions, and summarize for the group. More than anything else, the creative leader is responsible for maintaining an atmosphere of acceptance and openness, for permitting others to give their best. Respect of individual style and point of view are the rule of the day.

Creative people in business do not live in a vacuum, creating for their own pleasure. They have work to do. They need to be given the liberty to follow their instincts so that they can see the problem anew, and yet they need a sense of direction so that they will contribute something useful. It's possible in an attempt to make them accountable and productive to draw the reins too tight and stifle them.

Creative people need the stimulation of new challenges. It's often very productive to take a creative person out of design or public relations and have him spend a few days with the sales force or in marketing, contributing his point of view. This can be rewarding for everyone. In the new setting the creative person is seen as a visitor and is less self-conscious because he has fewer expectations to live up to. He is able to be more open in considering other people's problems than his own. Also the

173

people in the department he is visiting won't think of him as an expert and so his comments can be viewed innocently. Other workers are also inspired to think creatively by his example. Loaning creative people to other departments can lead to surprising and innovative results. It's worth a try when you're stuck.

Creative people are the future of the companies that employ them. They offer a way of thinking that looks at spaces and invents things to fill them. They see objects in new contexts and they adapt inventively to new situations where other people panic. Creative people are happiest when there are no signposts so they can walk on the grass and discover a shortcut.

The creative person's greatest gift is in raising the consciousness of the rest of the work force. He encourages others to develop their own creative strength. His devotion to himself is not an act of selfishness, but an involvement in his work. In every sense he is the best kind of worker. He accepts his work as his mission. He identifies with his goals and in his intention to create a new whole he expresses his feelings and proves his worth.

When you encourage the creative person, you encourage participation of others, productivity, individuality, and group spirit all at the same time.

SOME FINAL ADVICE

Your effectiveness in business comes from your effectiveness as a person. The two are inseparable.

To have a business goal worth pursuing implies that you have a life goal worthy of your best effort. No matter how much you understand about managing or being managed, motivating or fostering creativity, if you do not believe your work is meaningful you are unlikely to give your best.

Every person's work should do something to make this a better world. This is not a lofty dream, but a reflection of the truth of everyone's basic strivings. You want to do well so that you can have what you want: a safe home for your family, the ability to travel, the freedom to develop your talents, and the power to give those you love the choice to become their best. All of these goals for your personal world are meaningless unless the greater world of which we are all part is also safe and supportive.

You need to do your part in that larger effort by making your greatest contribution. It is only in giving as much as you can that you become your best, and it is only in being your best that you can be truly happy.

If you are the center of a happy, productive world, you are doing your part to make the world a better place.